Constable & Robinson Ltd
55–56 Russell Square
London WC1B 4HP
www.constablerobinson.com

First published in the UK by How to Books,
an imprint of Constable & Robinson Ltd, 2014

A copy of the British Library Cataloguing in Publication Data
is available from the British Library

ISBN: 978-1-84528-521-0 (paperback)
ISBN: 978-1-84528-559-3 (ebook)

1 3 5 7 9 10 8 6 4 2

Printed and bound in the EU

OWNER'S GUIDE TO A SMALL BUSINESS WEBSITE

WHAT YOU NEED AND HOW TO GET THERE – WITHOUT PAYING THE EARTH

Lisa Spann

CONTENTS

LIST OF FIGURES

PREFACE

This book is designed to help all small business owners to understand the basics of website design and to ensure that you – and your customers – are getting the best from your website. It doesn't matter if you are just starting out or have been trading for some time: this book will help you have an understanding of what you need to know about a website, whether you are designing and building it yourself or employing a web design agency to do it for you.

For example:

- Do you know if your website is compliant with the Equality Act?
- Do you know who owns your domain name? It may not be you!
- Do you have any idea about whether your website is working at its best for your business?
- Can you access your website, or is it totally out of your control?
- Do you know your front end from your back end or your CMS from your SEO?

All business owners should be in control of their own website as in many cases this is the first impression that a customer gets of you, your business and your service – and it needs to be right.

Having lots of 'bells and whistles' online is not always what is best for your business or your customers; you can end up wasting money and paying over the odds for a website that is simply not needed and not right for the job. Whether you are thinking of asking a family member or friend to design the website, or doing it yourself, you will need to know the basics of such aspects as search engine optimization (SEO) and how to ensure that your website complies with the relevant legal regulations, such as the Equality Act or the EU Cookies Directive.

Whoever you choose to design, build and host your website, you need to be in control since the quality of your website will impact directly on your livelihood.

Before deciding who to use to create your website, spend some time looking at your competitors' websites and working out what they do well and where they fall down. Compare not just the design but the functionality (how easy it is to get to where you want to go); count the clicks. Look at how easy (or not) it is to contact the business; do a Google search for their services (not their name) and see where they appear on the listing.

The more you know about your competitors' websites the more you can focus on what features/benefits your own website must (or must not) have.

The possibilities for designing and building a website are endless.

So many companies already have a web presence; indeed you may be one of them. Knowing what type of website you need – and the terminology used to describe and explain it – can get very confusing. One of the most important things to remember is future-proofing and subsequently the importance of having a content-managed website (see Chapter 1).

You will have to make lots of important decisions: for example, does your website have to be user-friendly if accessing through a smartphone, and is that what your potential customers are using? Do you want to sell your goods and services online? If you do, then you need to look at a form of e-commerce website and a whole host of associated options, including which payment gateway to use.

A great-looking website is one thing, but it must be built well to be sustainable, usable and legal.

Running your own business – in no matter what field – is both exciting and very hard work. As a business owner you are unlikely to be a marketing guru or web wizard. As such you will need to rely on other people to show you the way. The trick is to find someone who will point you in the right direction.

This book will guide you through important and, in some cases, crucial elements of designing and understanding a website, from what to ask your website designer in the first instance to who ultimately hosts it (and what that actually means). It will help you to avoid the common pitfalls that many small business owners fall into and to get the most from your website, whether you are doing it yourself or outsourcing to a specialist web design agency.

For those looking to recruit an in-house website designer, this book will give sound background information and some questions to ask at interview to ensure that the candidate really does know what they are talking about. Reading this book will give you a great overview of the subject.

Going forward it will be a useful point of reference. Although in the future technologies may change, the basic principles should remain the same.

1
UNDERSTANDING THE IMPORTANCE OF A GOOD WEBSITE

Every business, whether large or small, needs a good, well-built website that serves the needs of its customers. An extraordinarily large percentage of the world's population now has access to the internet, and countless statisticians have masses of data on global website usage. I have used a number of sources to put into context how many people use the internet, and this clearly demonstrates why having a good website is vital.

In 2012, over 87 per cent of the UK population had access to the internet (more than nine out of ten according to World Bank data). More detailed information about UK usage is available from the Office of National Statistics, and in February 2013 its latest report highlighted one very important point: in 2012, thirty-three million adults accessed the internet every day, more than double the 2006 figure of sixteen million, when directly comparable records began.

MAKING A GOOD FIRST IMPRESSION

In many cases the first impression someone gets of you and your business is via your website. If you do not have a website then there is a good chance that your competitors will get more enquiries simply based on the number of people who go online before looking elsewhere, such as in paper-based

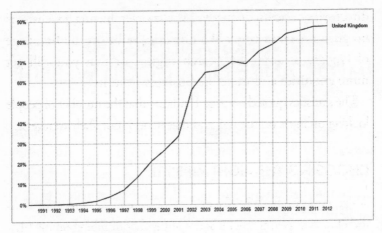

Internet users as a percentage of population[1]

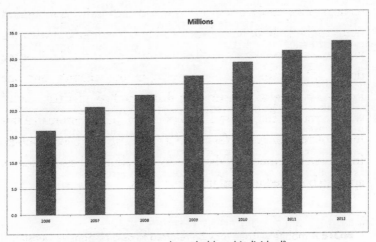

Internet access: household and individual[2]

1 https://www.google.co.uk/publicdata/explore?ds=d5bncppjof8f9_&met_y=it_net_user_p2&idim=country:GBR&dl=en&hl=en&q=statistics%20on%20uk%20internet%20usage

2 http://www.ons.gov.uk/ons/rel/rdit2/internet-access---households-and-individuals/2012-part-2/stb-ia-2012part2.html

directories or newspaper adverts. However, having a website is no guarantee that you will automatically be on the first page of Google or any other search engine, or that you will get more enquiries and therefore business from it.

The statistics quoted on page 1 indicate that the number of people looking online is on the rise, and that trend is not likely to reverse.

CHOOSING THE RIGHT WEBSITE

There are a number of different types of website and various reasons for a business having one. It is not always about selling online (that is just one option); more often than not it is about marketing your services to the public or other businesses. Each individual business needs to think about its end users first and foremost and what the website needs to do for them before working out the detail of the design. The main types are covered in this chapter, but one important thing to remember is that regardless of what sort of website you opt for, in virtually all cases you should ensure that it is in a content management system (CMS). Chapter 2 covers mobile-friendly websites and why these are essential, but the basic principles apply to both desktop and mobile websites.

> **NOTE** A mobile website may be referred to as a responsive website.

CONTENT MANAGEMENT SYSTEMS (CMS)

A content management system is more commonly known as a CMS and is a crucial element of any small business's website. A CMS simply allows you and your team to login and access the back end of the website to make changes as and when required without the need of web design skills. Updating news, testimonials, a gallery, contact information, opening hours and general text are all important when keeping your customers and potential customers up to date. Without access to a CMS, any changes required would need to be submitted by email to your web designer who would then quote for the work and schedule it in among their other commitments. Alternatively, if you have FTP (see Appendix 1) or similar access and understand HTML then you could do it yourself.

A good CMS will allow you to login and easily navigate around the content pages. Any content can be updated using a WYSIWYG ('What You See Is What You Get'); this looks like a typical word-processing tool with familiar icons that you will be used to, the only difference being is that it is online. The example on page 5 shows that you can bold, underline, insert images and align with similar icons to those used in standard word-processing products.

You may have a calendar of events that needs to be updated regularly. A simple module allows you to add and type without needing to understand any code or have any technical ability. The calendar example on page 5 is taken from a local website and shows just how easy it is to add an event. It should be a case of inputting basic information and then saving.

Most CMS are free as they are classed as 'open source' software that allows designers and developers to create add-ons and work together to make systems better. The examples shown are taken from CMS Made Simple.

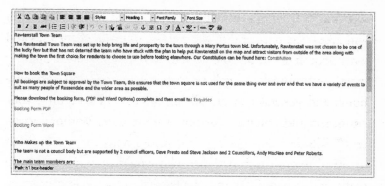

A standard user-friendly website interface with a content management system

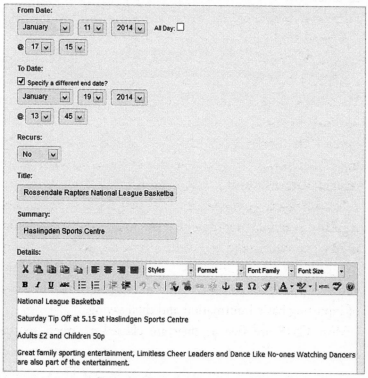

A standard easy-to-use calendar module

A SELECTION OF CMS SYSTEMS

This is the content management software that my team uses on a daily basis for our customers and has done so for a number of years. Before making the decision to use this, we evaluated a number of content management systems including the most common ones such as WordPress and Joomla. We opted for CMS Made Simple as it is very easy to use (the clue is in the name). As designers we write in code and then drop the code into a CMS so that anyone else can make amendments via a user-friendly interface. A CMS has got to be right for the end user, not the designer (who should not need one). There are some great add-on modules for this system and free themes that can be downloaded and installed if you are looking to build your own website.

WORDPRESS

This is probably the most well-known CMS and some website designers will only use this system. This is not to say, however, that it is the best option for everyone, or the easiest to use going forward. WordPress was originally known for blogging and has developed to be one of the main web software solutions for creating blogs and websites. Once again, it is free.

There are many templates within WordPress that can be simply downloaded and if you are having a go yourself then this is a good option. If you are looking to use a website designer, however, they too may use a template and say that it is bespoke, meaning that you will not get a website designed specifically with your needs in mind: do check. From my experience, people who are not designers and have tried to update their website using this CMS tool have struggled with it for a number of reasons, such as issues with the templates selected or not understanding all the different sections. Many website designers swear by it, but then they are likely to have the necessary technical skills.

One good thing about WordPress is that so many web developers all over the world are constantly adding modules and developing it, and more and more templates are being designed to work with it. Some are free, and some you need to pay for.

JOOMLA

Millions of people use this popular content management system. Again it is free to download and is open source, thus many designers and developers create modules to work with it.

Each CMS has its own communities and support groups, with their followers swearing that their system is the best. If you are using another designer or design agency, find out which they prefer to use and why. Ask them to show you it for real and see if you will be able to use it going forward. If you feel that it is not straightforward enough, say so and ask if there are other options.

> **TIP** Do not go with a system that you are not happy to use as this will turn out to be very frustrating and could be costly if you have to pay the designer to make changes later.

GENERAL CONTENT-DRIVEN WEBSITES

This is simply a website that carries lots of information about the company and the services it offers. These sites do not actively sell products directly to consumers via shopping carts, but encourage people to enquire further either through an enquiry form on the website or by telephoning. The majority of businesses, regardless of size, have this type of site; they provide information and may (or may not) generate income or direct enquiries for a product or service.

Some websites are informative and give credibility to a company, rather than sell a product or service. This is usually the case where the business is marketed through other sources such as networking or word of mouth, and the website acts as back-up. Equally parent companies use this kind of site to give an overview of their subsidiaries. In most cases, however, websites are intended to generate enquiries and therefore sales.

The development cost should be looked at as medium-term investment, as a good website should last a good few years (subject to any new technological advances that appear overnight). Compared to print advertising – leaflets or newspaper/magazine advertisements – a website should be far less costly and a much better investment.

HOW MUCH WILL IT COST?

This usually varies depending on the size of the site; the more pages of content, the more it is likely to cost to build. A small business with a budget of £500–1,000 plus VAT should be able (at current market rates) to get a very good website in a content management system that can grow as the business develops. You should be looking at having five pages of good content to get across what you have to say and offer, and for this £500 plus would be a very good price. Usually the price per page comes down as the number of pages goes up (assuming content pages), so £1,000 plus VAT would cover around twelve to fifteen pages.

The importance of content is covered in Chapter 6 on search engine optimization.

E-COMMERCE WEBSITES

An e-commerce website is simply a shopping website, which most people who have access to the internet will have used at some point. Many of the big high-street shops have seen a marked increase in sales via their online store; for example in early 2013, over 12 per cent of Debenhams' sales came from the internet, and this figure is rising.[3]

Online shopping sites are not just for the big companies; they are affordable for any local high street shop, regardless of what is being sold. It really doesn't matter what you sell or to whom; with a small investment you can have the best of both worlds. Some e-commerce software solutions may require the purchase of a licence, but this is not necessarily a bad thing. The free options may initially seem the best, but if you pay

---

3 http://www.telegraph.co.uk/finance/newsbysector/retailandconsumer/9788469/
   Debenhams-reveals-Christmas-discounting-battle-on-high-street.html

for the software there should be guaranteed support; and if this is your livelihood you want to make sure that the system you use is going to be reliable and current. In saying that, many of the free ones are excellent and provided by very large companies. As with general content management systems, these are open source, with developers the world over constantly creating modules for them.

Before embarking on an e-commerce website there are a number of points to consider and questions to be answered. Being fully informed before speaking with a designer will ease the process of finding the best solution for you and your circumstances.

SORTING THE DELIVERIES YOURSELF

This may seem obvious, but depending on the way you operate you may or may not hold stock; and if you are starting out you may or may not have room to hold stock. If you have a high street presence the chances are you are going to start by shipping any online orders yourself.

A good example of this is a local (to me) traditional sweet shop. They realized that there is a demand for buying sweets in bulk for weddings and parties and that they can supply just as well as any other online retailer. In addition, they specialize in American sweets and candy that they import and can ship anywhere in the UK. Having already got a web presence showing off what they did in terms of wedding favours and hampers, complete with opening times and so on, they progressed to an online shop where people can order online.

All the shipping is done in-house and they take payment through a set monthly priced payment gateway.

With any shop that ships in-house, the main issue is taking photos of the products and adding them to the database for the first time. Uploading is not difficult but it is time-consuming, and this should be taken into consideration when you are looking at the 'go live' date.

USING DROP SHIPPING

The other option for selling online is where you have suppliers that will ship for you (drop shipping). This is great if you sell lots of different items, and is commonly used when selling clothing. The other big advantage is that most suppliers will have the data that can be imported into the software that will run the site. There will still be some manual tweaking required as you will want to set your own prices and not simply use the recommended retail price (RRP), but this does speed up the process. It is also worth asking about images as some suppliers will provide them, but not in a way that can easily be tied up to the product, so time must be built in to do this. If this is the preferred option then it is worth asking your suppliers if they can send you a sample of the data for you to show to your website designer in advance. Again this can determine which software solution is right for you. This can also have an effect on the price

I worked with a fancy-dress shop that used this system; the owner has a high-street shop where she hires out costumes, and she decided to move online to sell certain items that went alongside her business, such as inexpensive masks that people wanted to buy rather than hire. We were provided with striking images that made the website look fabulous. The data was provided by the supplier and then imported into the site for the owner to amend. Unfortunately this did take some time; the images could not be supplied to tie in with the product data, which meant that the owner had to do some of the inputting.

Most design agencies will design and build the site for you, and I would expect them to set the categories and add a product to each category for you if you are shipping yourself. If you are using drop shipping then they will also input the data from your supplier. (Subject to it being in a useable form, of course.) What the agencies are not likely to do is the tweaking or the general data inputting, unless specifically agreed; they do not normally have the necessary resources for data inputting (further complicated by the fact that your selling prices will no doubt vary from the recommended retail price and you will have to decide how much you want to charge for each item).

PAYMENT GATEWAYS/MERCHANTS

A payment gateway is a service provider that authorizes payments for online retailers via e-commerce websites. There are many to choose from and each has its own way of charging: you can opt to pay per transaction with or without a monthly fee, or go for a monthly fee that covers all, or some other combination. Much of the decision comes down to the value of your products and how many you need to sell to cover this cost. If you are selling in a shop as well then the merchant that you are currently using may have a deal for taking online payments.

Two examples of payment gateways are:

- **PayPal** is probably the most well-known payment gateway, and people tend to either love it or hate it. Currently, there is not usually a set-up fee, but they do charge a percentage per transaction plus a small set transaction fee.
- **Payment Sense** offers capped monthly fees, which for some may be a better option especially if you want to budget for a set period of time.

There is no right or wrong option. Do some research and find out which payment gateway is best for your product. Then let your design agency know your choice as soon as you can so that they can ensure that their solution will work with it.

If you are looking to use a merchant, you will need to find out if your preferred supplier requires approval.

You will need to find out if the payment gateway of your choice requires approval. If you go down the PayPal route you do not require approval, as PayPal is a payment processor as opposed to a payment merchant; you can simply register and get going. For payment merchants such as Streamline, or any bank merchant services, however, you will need to apply and get approval.

It is wise to do this early in the process because the website designer will need to know who you will be using before embarking on the build, as different e-commerce tools work with different merchants and payment gateways.

DON'T FORGET!

Unlike non e-commerce websites, specific additional pages of information must be included in online shopping websites:

- **Privacy policy** It is important that you include a privacy policy as you are collecting personal data and more than likely using cookies (see Chapter 3). This should state what you use and store and where, and if you are going to share this data with any third party, who and what for, and give an opt-out option.

- **Delivery policy** As you will be selling items you need to ensure that you spell out any delivery charges clearly.

- **Returns policy** As with any sales, there are statutory rights which in this instance take into account distance selling rights. These give the buyer extra protection when purchasing over the internet. You must include a description, the price, the delivery/cancellation rights and information about the seller. Visit https://www.gov.uk/online-and-distance-selling-for-businesses for more information.

NOTE Do not copy these pages from someone else's website; you have no way of knowing if they have done the same and, if so, from which site in which country. If they have used information from a website in the USA, for example, it will not comply with UK or EU legislation.

HOW MUCH WILL IT COST?

For a small shop with eight to ten categories of products, and with any number of items within each category, the cost of the investment would be in the region of £1,500 plus VAT at current rates. This would give you a bespoke design, including the actual software that will run the site and the set-up of the initial system. I would expect all e-commerce solutions to come with search engine optimization included so that you can add your own title tags (see Chapter 6) and descriptions.

GENERAL WEBSITE WITH A SELLING OPTION

Depending on your business there may be a third option for you to consider. This is a general website but with an option to sell, but not through a true e-ecommerce system. There are three options worth mentioning:

- The first is for those selling, say, forty or fifty items and who are happy to use PayPal. A general CMS website will probably have its own shopping-cart solution that can be easily integrated into the website and designed to accommodate this number of items.
- The second is for those with even less to sell, say a handful of items or maybe a few chargeable downloads. Each one could simply be listed on a page linking to its own PayPal 'buy now' button.
- The third option is one we used for a local grocer who wanted his customers to be able to create their shopping list while browsing his products. He told us that most of his customers send a child with a list, or pop in on their way to work and leave a list to pick up on their way home. He realized that many more people who couldn't physically get to the shop

would like to do this, but that they could order online. The solution was to create a shopping list on the website that the end user emails to him along with contact information. He then calls the customer to arrange local delivery or collection and payment, which can either be over the phone using his shop card machine or cash on delivery/collection.

All these options are much quicker and cheaper initially to design and build as there is no payment integration required.

THINKING ABOUT THE DESIGN OF YOUR WEBSITE

The look of your website should represent you and your business and the way you operate. If your target market is the business sector then your website should be corporate, clean and efficient. A clear navigation is crucial as people – especially in business – will very quickly get bored of looking and move onto another supplier. Having one navigation bar at the top of the page with drop-down lists underneath each section is usually much better than having a main navigation and then a secondary one for the next section. Secondary navigations within sites can sometimes be the best option, but this is usually when sites are very large indeed and one navigation bar would be too cluttered.

Keep your corporate branding throughout and ensure that your logo is present and not altered to suit the site. The design should work around your branding, not the other way round. I once worked with a business where the previous designer decreed that their logo could not fit the design and therefore they had to change the logo. That should never be the case.

Always remember to make the design clear. When we use the internet we type in a question and are looking for a website that gives us the best answer (and, if applicable, at the best price). The public are very impatient and, if they can't navigate a website quickly, will rapidly move on.

Have some life on the home page, such as changing images or a corporate video. I suggest uploading videos to YouTube and embedding them into your website. YouTube is owned by Google and second to Google in the number of search results it returns, so from a search engine perspective this can only help. I would also recommend that you never have it set to autoplay as that can be very annoying and quite likely to deter someone from watching. Music can also put people off; I get very irritated when looking for something to suddenly have music playing and then have to scrabble about to find where to shut it up. This distracts from the reason I went to the website in the first place, and the first impression is not good.

Avoiding Flash

Something that should not be an issue for anyone starting out today, but that is still worth mentioning, is a type of design called Flash. This can sometimes be used to create really nice movement on a website, and is still used for creating online games. The downside is that it will not work on an iPhone or iPad and therefore should be avoided for the vast majority of business websites (unless you are in the gaming industry). Equally Google may not be able to read it and so you could lose potential enquiries. Similar effects can be created using HTML5, and most designers will now use this.

If your target market is the general public then Facebook/Twitter feeds on the home page are a very useful way of giving life and changing content to the website, as many of your customers will be posting frequently. Integrating one of the feeds is a good way of keeping content fresh and can also save on administration time. I would not normally have both Facebook and Twitter feeds as they usually end up saying the same thing and this can look a little silly – never mind repetitive – and slow the site down (more about this in Chapter 6).

Whatever your target market, if you are on any social media sites have links to them in the header or footers (LinkedIn as well as Facebook and Twitter). If you are in the hospitality trade, linking to and from TripAdvisor is a great add-on (providing you have good reviews to show off!).

HEADERS

The header of a website is usually where your logo will be, invariably positioned to the left; the right side is a useful area for some form of call to action. It is usually a good idea to have your telephone number and/or email address clearly shown within the header at the top of every page. You may also want to use this area for social media icons, or you may have a newsletter and want people to subscribe to it. The information is visible on all pages and is very user-friendly, so make the most of it.

FOOTERS

The footer is another great area for displaying elements that need to be on a website, but not necessarily aimed at the consumer. If you are an estate or letting agent, for example, you will be part of one of the ombudsmen schemes, in which case you will display their logo here with a link to their website. You may also have the logos of the property portals that you subscribe to here. If you belong to any affiliations or organizations, putting their logos and website links here gives great credibility to you and your business. This is also where links to privacy policies, terms and conditions and a sitemap are placed. Many of us never bother scrolling to the bottom of the page, but it is a great area to exploit.

This is also a good place to add any company registration information (it is a legal requirement if you are a registered company or charity in England and Wales to state your company registration number on your website).

Some websites list key phrases at the very bottom of the footer, such as:

Solicitors in Manchester | Conveyancing Services Manchester | Personal Injury Solicitors Manchester | Criminal Lawyers Manchester

This is to add extra relevant content and key phrases for the search engines to pick up on, and is fine as long as the text is not the same as the background colour; it must be visible to the end user.

A sitemap is mentioned within the search engine section as it is relevant for Google and the like, but having a link to a

HTML version in the footer is always a good idea if you have a large site so that a user can easily find the page they are looking for.

If the site is not too big, it is also worth using the footer for quick links to the pages to help the end user to navigate around the website easily.

HOME PAGE CONTENT

The main information on the home page should state what you do and where you do it. If you have got a lot to say then ensure that you set it out clearly, using informative subheadings. Avoid stating when you were established as no one is searching for that information and it is not the first thing they are looking for. Such information can go on an 'About Us' page if you are having one; if you are not (to help keep costs down) have the 'About' section further down the home page so that if someone wants to read it they can, but it is not the first thing they see.

Chapter 6 (on search engine optimization) will cover more about the importance of headings and subheadings as these are important for Google. However, they are also very important for visitors to the website. When we read newspaper articles we look at the headings and subheadings first, to get an idea as to whether something is of interest or not. It is the same with a website: if a heading is clear and relevant, it will draw the eye and encourage the user to read on.

TIP Avoid having the words 'Welcome' or 'Home' as the main heading on the home page. No one will be using a search engine to find you or what you do using either of these words; stick to what is relevant. For example, the main heading on the home page for a travel agent could be 'ABC Travel Agents, Anytown'; this clearly states who you are, what you do and where, to both the end user and the search engines. See Chapter 6 for more information.

CONSIDERING THE NEEDS OF THE END USER

The end user is the person you need to satisfy and impress; you need them to stay on your website and engage with you. Always have them at the forefront of your mind when planning the design and build of your website. It is not about what *you* want to say, it is about what *they* want to hear/read.

When we use search engines we are looking for an answer to a question; be it 'Chinese takeaway in town' or 'Lemon cheesecake recipe', we are expecting the search engine to find us a list of relevant answers. The search engine's job is to put those answers in what it sees as the best set of results. The question we ask and how specific it is will determine the results that are given and the order in which they are shown.

Say a member of the public is looking for a solicitor in a local town. They are likely to enter in a search engine 'solicitors in Anytown'. The set of results that they will probably see will include some that have created a Google Place (see

Chapter 6) and then a list of other solicitors in the area. In many cases people click on a couple and then realize that solicitors offer different services, so at this point they may refine their search and be more specific. The person searching already knows what type of solicitor they are looking for, i.e. a criminal solicitor, a specialist in family law or a personal injury lawyer. If the practice offers all of these then the home page needs to be clear and directional so that the end user can click onto the more detailed information page required.

If all the information is crammed into one or two pages, people will be put off and simply not stay to read through it all to find the bit they want. This is not to say, however, that your website needs hundreds of pages with just one paragraph of text on each one. Simply think about the key services that you offer and, if you have lots of relevant information to display, allocate a full page to each one; and if you have a few services that sit together comfortably, collate those onto one page.

On an e-commerce website the home page can have special offers and enticing products, but if someone is looking for something specific keep the categories clear and easy to find. I would always recommend the inclusion of a search box to help the end user speed up their search if they know what they are looking for.

For example, if you are selling a wide range of clothing to the public and offer menswear, ladies' wear, children's wear, shoes, accessories and so on, you list the main categories and then subcategories. For ladies' shoes this might mean heels, sandals and boots, etc. A customer will have to make quite a few clicks before getting close to what they are looking for. If the customer knows she wants (some red heels, perhaps), she can type these words into a search box. It will search the site for the shoes that match, thus speeding up the process and keeping the consumer engaged. Making the user experience easier will encourage them to stay and browse, and hopefully buy.

Contents pages on a shopping site are usually linked to at the bottom of the website. Many of the contents pages are quite boring but important, covering terms and conditions, delivery, contact and privacy etc. These pages are not the first things that someone is going to be looking for (or interested in) so do not need to be within the main navigation of the site.

If you are a small high street retailer and are not selling many items, consider having a dual site that shows off your services and your physical shop as well as the online shop. This is a very good option for getting the best of both worlds and is no more expensive than simply having the e-commerce part.

2
THE GROWING IMPORTANCE OF MOBILE-FRIENDLY WEBSITES

Back in August 2011, Ofcom reported that a third of all adults in the UK use a smartphone, which can be interpreted as one third of your potential customers![4] More recently (February 2013), the Office of National Statistics stated two key points:[5]

- Access to the internet using a mobile phone more than doubled between 2010 and 2012, from 24 per cent to 51 per cent.
- In 2012, 32 per cent of adults accessed the internet every day from a mobile phone.

As with general internet usage, these figures are only going to increase and, it appears, at an exponential rate.

WHAT IS A 'MOBILE WEBSITE'?

A mobile website/mobile-friendly website is one that is designed specifically to work on a smartphone such as an iPhone, Samsung Galaxy, Blackberry, etc – sometimes referred to as a responsive site. Although most websites will technically work on a smartphone, the end user is less likely to use the site if they have to stop, put a drink or a bag down

---

4 http://www.bbc.co.uk/news/technology-14397101
5 http://www.ons.gov.uk/ons/dcp171778_301822.pdf

and use two fingers to scroll and make the visual area larger so that they can see what is there. This is far from being user-friendly, and in some instances is just unusable.

> **NOTE** If you have an existing website and it is quite old and uses a technology called Flash, it will not work on an iPhone or iPad (see Chapter 1). In future this may change, but it is outdated and the technology has been replaced by HTML5.

MOBILE DESIGN

A mobile-friendly version of a website keeps the same branding and theme as the main desktop site but is adjusted to have a vertical menu (usually) with easy-to-use buttons for fingers. It is a design made specifically to fit the smartphone screens and with relevant information for someone on the go. Not all content needs to be displayed on a mobile version, but if you have a shop and people visit then contact information, a map and opening hours are crucial; your terms of delivery, however, are less important.

Much greater use is made of graphics as opposed to words to help people navigate the site; remember the old adage – 'a picture speaks a thousand words.'

WHY HAVE A MOBILE WEBSITE?

A normal website is built to work on a PC, laptop or tablet computer and is often just as big when viewed on a smaller screen.

This means the text can be difficult to read and requires the user to zoom in and pan around the web page to read it properly.

I always tell businesses to load up their website on their phone and see what it looks like. Most haven't done this before and so have no idea of any issue that their customers or potential customers may be experiencing.

As you would expect, some industries have more need of a mobile-friendly version of their website than others. For example, a locksmith is an ideal candidate as their customers could very well be locked out of their house or place of work and only have their phone to hand as a means of getting help!

Another industry where this is very relevant is property. Estate and letting agents need to have a mobile version for ease of searching their properties online. If someone is looking to buy or rent a property, it is usual practice to drive to the area that they are interested in and see what is available. Upon seeing an agent's board they may require more information – especially the price – and there is a strong possibility that, using their smartphone, they will try to find it on the agent's website. If that website is not mobile-friendly then it will become a very frustrating task. Now imagine that there is a property on the same road with a different agent. The potential buyer then looks for that agent's website and it is mobile-friendly… If they are looking to view, the mobile-friendly version is most likely to be their first choice. Some estate agents and letting agents use QR (Quick Response) Codes on their 'For Sale' and 'To Let' boards. These are scanned by a smartphone application that then directs the end user to that property page on their website. If this does not direct to a mobile version it is of little use.

My final example is of a high street shop or service provider where clients are likely to visit. Customers will be out and about looking to see who is open and when, and also where they are in the town. If you park up in a central car park and then need to find the location, a mobile version will show a clearer map and usually a phone number that can easily be pressed to call for more information if necessary.

As more and more people use mobile phones to access the internet, this is going to become increasingly relevant. All businesses need to think of how their clients, both new and old, access their websites, and be prepared to adapt to their needs.

Another reason to consider a mobile-friendly version is if your employees are frequently out of the office and need to access key information from your website, such as PDF documents or perhaps technical information on a specific product or service. If your website contains a lot of technical data then having a mobile-friendly version will help them look professional and efficient by quickly accessing what they need to know.

WEB APPS V APPS

A mobile-friendly website is sometimes referred to as a Web App (Web Application). This is different to an App that is downloaded from an App store or equivalent.

A number of businesses go down the road of having mobile Apps developed for them and whereas it is true to say that Apps have a place, personally I think Apps are for offline content such as games and saving discount vouchers etc. For a business to consider an App you must consider both the devices and their operating systems. There is Apple with the iPhone, then the Android App Store and the Windows App Store, and then Blackberry. Apps need to be developed for all platforms and some are not that easy. They all need to be maintained for all platforms and when they update you need your App updating to work too, and this can become very costly.

There are specialist App developers who are great at what they do, but do think about whether it is really worth going down this route – and, most importantly, what your end users want from you. The cost implications also need to be considered as a true App will cost much more than a mobile-friendly website. In essence, a mobile version of your website (Web App) is just that: a mobile version with the same information but in an accessible way on all platforms. Also, if you update the content on your main website then in most cases the mobile version will be updated at the same time.

HOW MUCH WILL IT COST?

A mobile website costs no more than a normal-sized website, because they are very similar. The content from a desktop website can be reused and the established branding can also be used in the design. However, having desktop and mobile websites created at the same time will be more cost-effective and produce an easier-to-maintain product than if done separately. Speak with your designer at the start of the process and explain that you would like a mobile-friendly version too; since this requires a different design the overall cost will increase, but will be well worth the initial investment.

UNDERSTANDING THE BENEFITS OF A MOBILE WEBSITE

Here is a short list of just some of the advantages of having a mobile-friendly website:

- It allows visitors to view and browse a website easily while on the move, without needing to zoom in and out of the site to view certain sections.
- User guides can be downloaded straight to the user's phone.
- A business can make its opening times available much more easily.
- Restaurants can include their menus, with links to booking services or the option to call straight from the website to check availability.
- Estate agents and letting agents can make their property listings much more usable on a mobile phone, making browsing properties a far more enjoyable experience without access to a PC.
- A business can make its contact information more prominent, including a map for directions. It's even possible to get a user's current location to provide directions.

- There is also a very good chance that Google and no doubt other search engines will have a different set of results if you search on a mobile device than if you search on a desktop. I would not be surprised if before very long the search results on a smartphone will be shown in the order of those with a mobile version first.

- QR Codes could be provided that, once scanned with a smartphone, direct the user to a specific mobile page with more information about a product or service.

NOTE A QR (Quick Response) Code is the trademark for a type of barcode that consists of (traditionally) black modules (square dots) arranged in a square grid on a white background, which can be read by application software that can be freely downloaded to smartphones. You can now create your own for free online, and for a small payment you can have a coloured version with your own branding, as shown below.

A personalized QR (Quick Response) Code

EXAMPLES OF MOBILE-FRIENDLY WEBSITES

The following examples of mobile-friendly websites alongside their main desktop versions will give you an idea of the differences between the two. As you will see from both the large website of Wikipedia through to the smaller business websites, the principles are the same. The navigation must be made to work vertically on a mobile version as opposed to the horizontal set-up of a desktop version. Equally on a smaller vertical screen the buttons must be finger-friendly.

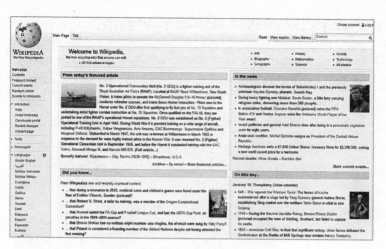

Wikipedia screenshot on a laptop computer

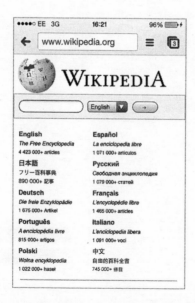

The same Wikipedia website viewed on an iPhone

A Kent-based estate agent's website viewed on a laptop

The same estate agent's website
viewed on an iPhone

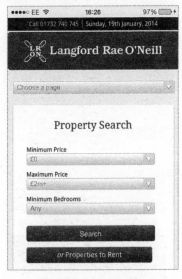

The estate agent's property
search designed to be user-friendly
on a smartphone

A dance school's website viewed on a laptop

The same website viewed
on an iPhone (left)

The same website viewed
on an iPhone (right)

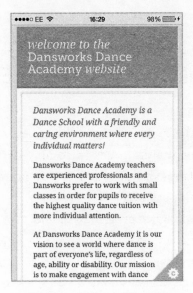

Another view of the dance school's
website on a smartphone

3
UNDERSTANDING
THE LEGAL REQUIREMENTS

It seems that the majority of small business owners are not aware that their website needs to comply with certain legal rules and regulations. Although there are not many of these, compliance is importance.

The website designer or agency should take this on board on behalf their client, but in many cases – especially where a business owner chooses to do it themselves or gets a friend of a friend who is good at design to do it for them – this is either simply not known or taken into account.

The legal requirements of a website are not difficult to comply with; much of it is basic common sense, and with any well-built website is easy to achieve. Furthermore, it should come as a standard part of the build and never increase the overall cost.

THE EQUALITY ACT: WHAT IS IT ALL ABOUT?

This legislation has been in place since 2002 when an amendment to the Disability Discrimination Act was made to include websites (among other areas). The Disability Discrimination Act was then brought into the Equality Act 2010, but the principle remains the same. Although this legislation is specific to the United Kingdom, other countries have similar guidelines, and from a website perspective compliance with the UK regulations is more than likely going to mean compliance with the United States, for example. In the online world you can have clients from anywhere, and as such the basic principles apply.

The basic principle of this Act with regard to a website is that as a business you must make *reasonable effort* to ensure that your website is suitable for the visually impaired. Online this can include someone who has difficulty reading small letters right through to a blind person using the internet via a screen reader, and everything between. Initially you may be wondering how is someone who is blind able to use the internet? Screen readers are specifically designed to read out loud what they see on a website and this is why ensuring that any website is well built and takes this into account is so important.

The Equality Act is there to ensure that no one is left out and discriminated against, and as a business owner you would not want to miss out on a potential sales market!

ENSURING YOUR WEBSITE COMPLIES

Images and pictures

As previously stated, the basic principle is to make a reasonable effort and the best way to achieve this is to ensure that every image/graphic/logo/box etc. has a description behind it so that a screen reader can interpret it.

For example, if there is a photo of you on your website then we would all be able to see who it is in relation to any text supplied on the same page. A screen reader would identify that it was a picture; but unless the code behind identified that person as you, neither the screen reader (and therefore the end user) would have any idea. Equally, if you have a random image such as your logo, you do not need to describe the colours or the image, rather just state that this is the company logo.

Images are used on websites to give life and help break up words, but they are also used as logos, advertisements and buttons. If a screen reader doesn't know that a picture is actually a button that 'does' something, the person using it will not be able to navigate around the site. This is where discrimination comes in.

The simplest way to ensure a website makes reasonable effort is to ensure that all images and graphics are described in the code behind them. This is the one thing that many website designers fail to do, and yet it is so easy.

TIP Search engines cannot read pictures and images unless you describe them; search engines like to 'read'.

Fonts and colours

All business owners want to offer the best possible service to their clients, and the online website is often the first impression someone gets of a business. Ensuring that a screen reader can read images is one thing, but for others it may be that clashing colours or font size is an issue. Once again there are a number of options which should be standard for all professional website designers:

- Choose a clear font; you may think it is boring, but having a fancy script font will not help the end user, especially if they have issues with their eyesight.
- Choose a good size; do not try and cram lots of text on a page to avoid scrolling. Think more creatively and have clear tabs within a page so that the font size can be easily read and seen by all.
- Avoid a pale grey font on a light background. You do not have to use black: it can be a dark blue, or charcoal grey – just keep it clear.
- Colours can be tricky. If your branding has already been done then you do not have to change it to suit those with colour-blindness, for example, but online try to use your colours in headings and buttons rather than having coloured fonts on coloured backgrounds, making it hard to read.

There are online tools available to test such things; a good one is leaverou.github.io/contrastio, with which you can set the font and background colours (simply type red, green, blue, etc) and it will tell you how easy it is to read, and then make any necessary adjustments. With regard to the contrast ratio rate, the guide is to be at least 4.5:1 (i.e. four and a half to one). You can set the font and background colours and be told how easy it is to read, and then make any necessary adjustments.

As I said earlier, much of this comes down to common sense. Do remember the standard is *reasonable effort* so if your corporate colours are red and green and someone is red/green colour-blind, then it would be unreasonable to expect you to rebrand to accommodate them.

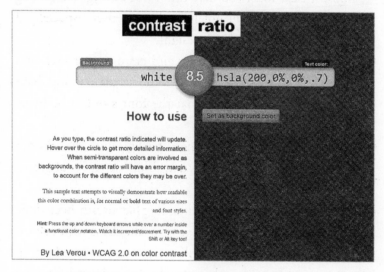

Contrast ratio shows the difference between using a dark background and a light background

EU COOKIES DIRECTIVE

This relatively new piece of legislation from May 2011 has been enforced in the UK from May 2012 and covers all websites based in the EU. There is also a question over whether it should be implemented if the website is held outside the EU but aimed at the people within the EU. My view would be to make it comply as it is not that hard.

You may not know what this is, but I am in no doubt that you will all have had some experience of it. When you go to a website for the first time, you may see a banner at the top or a pop-up or a box appear that says this site uses cookies.

We use cookies to ensure that we provide you with a good experience on our website, read more or click the button to accept   Close

Standard cookie message pop-up box

Alternate cookies pop-up box, usually from the footer

Most people will simply click OK or continue to move to where they want to go. It is, however, the legal responsibility of the business owner to ensure that if the website uses cookies, the end user is notified as soon as they get to the site and are clearly directed to what is used and why.

WHAT ARE COOKIES?

A cookie in computer terminology is a small piece of code that is stored on a web server that remembers small amounts of information about the user viewing that website.

Cookies can be very useful, and are often used when you login to a website such as online banking; basically it is a cookie that remembers your username. Similarly, if you browse on an online shop and next time you go back it remembers what you last viewed, a cookie has enabled this.

Cookies are also sometimes used to make certain things work on a website such as Facebook, YouTube and Twitter integration. One of the common uses of cookies is Google Analytics (see Chapter 6). Google Analytics tracks the type of visitor coming to your site, where they are from, what internet browser they use – such as Internet Explorer, Firefox or Chrome – and whether they are using a desktop or a mobile phone. Google Analytics also records how long someone stays on your website and what pages they looked at; all very useful information to a business, and all requiring a cookie. Cookies are good things, not bad.

If you use cookies then you must direct the end user to your privacy policy and explain what you used and why. This is a legal requirement, as the end user must have the right to leave your website without any of their data being captured. The pop-up box or the banner must have the option to change settings or decline, and the code behind this needs to action accordingly.

Neither of these is difficult to implement and should never increase the cost of a website as they *must* be done.

THE ADVERTISING STANDARDS AUTHORITY (ASA)

This is not so much a legal requirement but something that as a business owner you need to be aware of when writing the content for your website. The Advertising Standards Authority governs what you can say on your website, Facebook and

Twitter pages and e-marketing shots in the UK. It also covers other forms of marketing advertisement such as billboards and leaflets, which are outside the scope of this book.

Their own website states:

'The Advertising Standards Authority is the UK's independent regulator of advertising across all media. We apply the Advertising Codes, which are written by the Committees of Advertising Practice. Our work includes acting on complaints and proactively checking the media to take action against misleading, harmful or offensive advertisements.'

In many cases the people who are most likely to report you are, of course, your competitors.

WHAT DOES THIS MEAN TO YOU?

Many businesses are not aware that their websites, Facebook pages and Twitter feeds are governed by the ASA (www.asa.org.uk). Each week rulings are published plus the full details of the complaint and why the decision that was made was given. I have a lot of time for the organization although I can't always say that I agree with the guidelines that are adhered to – some just take common sense out of the equation – but in such cases it is the guideline that is wrong, not the enforcement of it. What I do like is that it doesn't matter whether you are a small, medium or large business: if you breach a guideline you will be brought to task.

In order not to fall foul of the ASA, the most important thing to remember is not to mislead your clients/potential clients. You can only say you are the best or the busiest or the only one to offer something if you can prove it!

Having followed the rulings on the ASA for some time, I find that the main problems that come up with website rulings include businesses saying they are 'Number One' in their area when they can't then back up the statement; or a health-based industry claiming that a product or service will help some ailment without having any scientific proof to substantiate it.

TIP Remembering Carlsberg's 'probably the best lager in the world': this 'probably' goes a long way towards understanding how to avoid potential problems.

Case study

If you have won awards then shout about them – but only if they are genuine! In the vast majority of cases a business would not dream of saying they had won an award if they hadn't, but every now and again it does happen. The same rules apply to any product that you have made or are selling; if it has not won an award then you cannot say it has.

In the case of marketing, the definition of the word 'award' really means that the award is from an independent organization in competition with similar products or businesses.

A good example of a ruling that was upheld by the ASA was in March 2012 against Ergoflex Ltd.[6] The complaint related to the company's website back in August 2011. There was one complainant with two points, who questioned whether one could be substantiated:

---

6 http://www.asa.org.uk/Rulings/Adjudications/2012/3/Ergoflex-Ltd/SHP_ADJ_169172.aspx

'a. The website ergoflex.co.uk stated "Award winning mattresses from only £229". Underneath the text "As seen in", the logos for the following media appeared in rotation: the *Mail on Sunday*, the *Telegraph*, the *Observer*, the *Daily Mail*, *House Beautiful*, the *Sunday Times*, *4 Homes*, and *Channel 4*.'

The response from the defendant was:

'Ergoflex said the references to awards related to a review of their product on an independent review website. On the home page of the website, text stated "Check out our Current 5-Star Award Winner" and a box underneath, which stated "MEMORY FOAM BUYERS' GUIDE BEST BUY *****" linked to a review of an Ergoflex mattress. Text at the end of the review stated "Taking every aspect into account... the Ergoflex memory foam mattress receives our 5-star award." Under the text "AWARD WINNER", a rosette-shaped icon had the text "BEST BUY" written on it.'

The ASA ruled against the company by saying that the end user would believe that an award meant they had gone head-to-head with other products of a similar nature and won. Their response was:

'The ASA considered consumers would interpret the claim to mean that Ergoflex's mattresses had won an award, in competition with similar products under set rules and criteria, given by an independent organization. While we noted the review website referred to Ergoflex as an award winner, we noted we had not seen evidence that Ergoflex's mattresses had won an award, in competition with similar products, given by an independent organization. Furthermore, we considered that a positive product review did not constitute an "award" as consumers would understand it. We concluded the claim was misleading'.[7]

---

7   http://www.asa.org.uk/Rulings/Adjudications/2012/3/Ergoflex-Ltd/SHP_ADJ_169172.aspx

FACEBOOK AND TWITTER

Social media sites are used by businesses as either an add-on to the general marketing or in some cases as a replacement for a website. The same rules apply in terms of what you can say about yourself, your company or products on these pages as on a website.

Many businesses are not aware that the ASA also governs another area that is popular with social media sites, and that is competitions and giveaways. A popular way to increase likes or get more followers is to offer a free giveaway when a certain number of likes/followers are achieved. As with any competition in any format, terms and conditions must be set and must comply with the set guidelines. With Facebook and Twitter this applies even if it is just a free giveaway.

The Committees of Advertising Practice (CAP) write and maintain the UK Advertising Codes, which the Advertising Standards Authority then administers. Any giveaways and competitions come under certain CAP codes that specify the timely manner in which prizes should be received by winners and how the prizes are administered.

Case study

An example of this is a ruling that was upheld in December 2012, where a small company offered a Twitter giveaway: 'Follow and win a Kindle.' The winner in this case had not received the prize and questioned the giveaway. The ASA upheld the complaint as the CAP code required that prize promotions must specify before or at the time of entry the date by which prizewinners would receive their prizes, if more than thirty days after the closing date.

E-SHOTS

Email marketing is a cost-effective method for any business to get their message across to a large number of people very quickly. There are guidelines on spamming and you must always ensure there is an unsubscribe option, but in addition to those you must also ensure that you do not make any claims that cannot be substantiated.

Case study

This is an example of a ruling that was upheld over an email advert in January 2013.[8] The email advert was in regard to a body cream that claimed to reduce cellulite fast and that the end user could look like an A-list celebrity. Someone questioned whether the claims were exaggerated.

The company produced some information about the two active ingredients which they thought substantiated it. The ASA ruled that as the information provided was limited and could not prove that the cream could make a consumer look like the A-lister mentioned, the claim was basically exaggerated. This particular email breached four CAP codes: rules 3.1 (Misleading advertising), 3.7 (Substantiation), 3.11 (Exaggeration) and 12.1 (Medicines, medical devices, health-related products and beauty products).

---

8 http://www.asa.org.uk/Rulings/Adjudications/2013/1/Rodial-Ltd/SHP_ADJ_210708.aspx

AVOIDING BAD PUBLICITY

As a business you must ensure that you do not mislead the public in any way or imitate and pretend to be connected to any large organization when you are not.

Case study

A good example of this was with Mazda UK Ltd's website. The website www.mazda-uk.co.uk stated at the top of every page: 'Mazda UK. We are a direct outlet for main dealer part exchanges, ex-lease and company vehicles.' The name Mazda UK was flanked on either side by an image of wings reminiscent of those in the Mazda Motors UK Ltd logo.

The basis of the issue is that the banner implied that they were connected to Mazda Motors UK Ltd (Mazda Motors) and that they took unfair advantage of the reputation and trademark of the Mazda Motor Company's name. Mazda Motors UK Ltd, a subsidiary of Mazda Motor Corporation of Japan, challenged the advert and it was upheld. This advert breached two CAP codes: rules 3.1 (Misleading advertising) and 3.43 (Imitation and denigration).[9]

Many more examples are available on the ASA website. If you are in any doubt about any claim, make sure that you can substantiate what you say.

---

9 http://www.asa.org.uk/Rulings/Adjudications/2012/12/Mazda-UK-Ltd/SHP_ADJ_205706.aspx

W3C: WORLD WIDE WEB CONSORTIUM

Again this is not strictly a legal requirement but is something to be aware of, especially if you are looking to build your own website (or using a friend of the family to do it for you).

The World Wide Web Consortium (W3C)[10] is an international community where member organizations, a full-time staff and the public work together to develop Web Standards led by web inventor Tim Berners-Lee. W3C's mission is to lead the web to its full potential.

These great people create, maintain and update the standards that all website designers should comply with. In the same way builders comply with building standards and regulations to ensure a property is sustainable and fit for purpose, this is the World Wide Web's equivalent.

Our industry changes very quickly as new smarter/quicker ways of accessing the web are being developed. The languages that are used to build a website are regularly updated and guidelines on how to use these languages are given by W3C.

I look at this in more detail in Chapter 3 but you can easily check your own website and see how it fares by going to the W3C Validator online (http://validator.w3.org) and entering your home page. Check all your website pages as each one will have different elements that may be good or bad. This is a free service and the results are instant.

---

10 http://www.w3.org

4
UNDERSTANDING DOMAIN NAMES

This chapter covers the different types of domain names, how to ensure that they are registered in the correct name and why this is so important. Domain names can get very technical but for the purposes of this book I am looking at the daily practical side of knowing the basics rather than getting involved in setting them up, managing the different elements or the ways in which to transfer them.

WHAT IS A DOMAIN NAME?

Firstly, it is important to explain what a domain name is. Many people think it is www.mywebsiteaddress.co.uk, but it isn't: a domain name is what comes *after* the www., so in this example mywebsiteaddress.co.uk. It is worth noting that once the www. prefix is added, many people describe this as a URL (uniform resource locator).

A domain name is a user-friendly/memorable way for people to access a website and also the basis for company/professional email addresses. Once you have a domain name you can set up any number of email addresses on it, such as John@..., enquiries@... etc.

The domain can also be used in the back-end set-up of email accounts in mail clients such as Microsoft Outlook as the mail server information; basically if you are setting up your email accounts there will be fields asking for your domain name, so it is useful to know what to put in there: the bit after the www. or @.

DIFFERENT TYPES OF DOMAIN NAME

Domain names are quite structured and there are some restrictions as to who can register what, but without getting too much into technical detail the following information should give a good overview as to what you and your business should look to register and why.

In some countries you must be based there to register the extension of that country. A good example is the Isle of Man; you need to have an office or outlet there to register an extension of .co.im. Note, however, that anyone anywhere can register .co.uk and .com addresses. There are many options available but I am only going to look at some of the most common ones here. Many businesses will register more than one domain name which is fine, but only one will be submitted to the search engines; the others will direct traffic to the main domain name.

.CO.UK

Most businesses operating in the United Kingdom will register a domain name that ends in .co.uk. There are a couple of reasons for this: .co.uk simply stands for a company in the UK, and identifies to the end user that the company is based there. This is also one of the cheapest options open to a business within the UK, and can now be registered for up to ten years at a time. Most consumers in the UK searching via Google.co.uk, for example, will assume that a website on a .co.uk domain name is the one they are looking for in the first instance.

.COM

These domain names are normally used by international companies, American companies (they also have the option of .us) and those companies based anywhere else that could not get the .co.uk or national equivalent. In saying that, many smaller businesses will normally register the .com to prevent any competitor doing so and use it to direct people to their own website. Again these can be registered from one year plus at a time, but as they are available to many more people their value is higher and, as such, will cost more than a .co.uk. If you are in a highly competitive industry, the cost of having both is usually worth it.

.CO

This domain extension is relatively new as until 2010 this would indicate that the company was in Columbia, but regulations were changed allowing larger companies to shorten their domain name and it became an option worldwide. Once again this is not as cheap as registering a .co.uk domain name and is on a par with a .com. This has not really taken off yet in marketing terms but is a good option if you are struggling to get your preferred name.

.UK.COM

This is another good option if you are starting out and cannot get a .co.uk or .com with either your company name or what you do within it. They work in the same way as a .com but are usually much more expensive.

.ORG AND .ORG.UK

These are usually registered by organizations (not-for-profit businesses); again this indicates to the end user what type of company or organization they are dealing with. The .org.uk is an equivalent of a .co.uk and any organization based in the UK can register one; the cost is on a par with a .co.uk. The .org is the international equivalent, i.e. on a par with .com and, as such, can be slightly more expensive.

.LTD AND .LTD.UK

As the name suggests, ideal for Limited companies. In many cases, if you register one of these you do need to associate the Limited company's registration number with it.

Here are a few other domain extensions that you may come across or want to consider:

- **.biz** These can be registered by anyone anywhere and are not country specific. The intention for this top-level domain extension was for businesses but in the UK they are not the first choice.

- **.net** This extension is short for network and is one of the first top-level domain names to be created. Originally for those companies involved with technology such as internet providers, they are open for anyone to buy and use.
- **.co.im** As mentioned on page 52, this is the extension for the Isle of Man and can only be registered directly with Domicilium (IOM) Limited and is intended solely for the use of those based on the Isle of Man.
- **.ac.uk** This is used by higher education institutions across the UK and associations linked to them (there are many more like this including .gov.uk, and police.uk – most of which are self-explanatory and not for regular business use).

CHOOSING THE RIGHT DOMAIN NAME – AND DECIDING HOW MANY

There are so many options to choose from and this can become a big issue in the future, so before rushing in think about it. If you are starting a business it is certainly worth looking at what domain names are available before the company name is chosen and registered. The two do not have to be the same but, at time of writing, I am aware of a local business owner who is currently defending his right to use his domain name against a Limited company that registered that exact name as their company name with Companies House. Not every business needs to be a Limited company to register a domain name, so if you are a sole trader or registered your own Limited company in a name different to the chosen domain name, beware!

You can register any domain name that you like as long as no one else has already got it, and subject to the information mentioned earlier. In the scheme of things, domain names are not very expensive to register so many companies do buy more than one. The usual practice is for most to register the different variants such as the .co.uk and the .com, but if you have a name that could be spelt incorrectly then a variant of the spelling could be worthwhile. There is also the option of registering a domain name pertaining to what you do, such as EstateagentsinEngland.co.uk.

Although domain names may be relatively inexpensive to register initially, the more you have the more it will add up and can end with being a waste of money. Having lots of domain names does not mean that your website or web presence will be better than a business that just has one; it can just mean higher renewal bills. From a search engine perspective, having fifty different domain names all pointing to the same content on the same website is not helpful either; Google are a little cleverer than that and will not fall for that trick. Getting more than one domain name is not going to improve your search engine optimization.

Search engines do need to be taken into account when choosing a domain name unless this particular area of marketing is a very small one for your business. Basically, there are two ways of looking at it:

- If you are having a website to back up other marketing campaigns such as press, leaflet drops and networking and as a source of credible information, then you would stick with your company name. Each page can then be optimized accordingly based on the content and friendly URLs can be added (see Chapter 6).

- If, however, being found on Google is very important for you, then thinking about the name that is to be used and submitted to the search engines is very important. This is just one element of search engine optimization but one worth taking seriously.

When choosing a domain name always think about the end user and spelling. If it gets too long they may end up somewhere completely different because of a simple typing error. Equally, if you are using the same domain name for emails, and therefore adding enquiries@ in front of it, you could end up actually losing said enquiries through mistyping.

USING HYPHENS

Some people do not like the thought of having a hyphen (-) in their domain names. If you fall into that category, pause for a moment before dismissing the idea completely. A hyphen in a domain name is just like a space between words. It is a great option if the main domain without hyphens has been taken already. Naturally, as mentioned above, you do have to take into consideration the length, and having lots of hyphens in a domain name can be problematic from the end user's perspective.

Hyphens can also be very useful if you have a company name where one word merges into another and does not read very clearly. For example, if I had a business called Someone's Estates, the domain of someonesestates.co.uk could play tricks on the eyes due to the 'eses' in the middle. This would be better split into someones-estates.co.uk for ease of use and clarity.

In the past it was seen as a good thing to have hyphens in a domain with Google, as the hyphen was classed to be the same as a space within words – but things change. It is no longer seen as a positive, but equally it is not a negative; remember the domain name is just one element that Google looks at.

USING KEYWORDS

As already mentioned, the shorter the domain name the better for the end user. Although the domain name is just one element that search engines take into account, its form is still relevant.

You can, for example, register two domain names: one that is keyword-rich and quite long that is submitted to the search engines, and one that is abbreviated for business cards, email addresses and signage etc. for the end user to enter easily. Both will go to the same website and the end user is not likely to see the change in the URL at the top of the page when the domain name redirects to the longer one.

An example of this could be an estate agent based in a Verylongtownname. A good domain that helps with search engines could be verylongtownnameestateagents.co.uk; this would be keyword-rich but very long and, if you add enquires@ to the front, is not user-friendly at all. However, an abbreviated version could be vltnea.co.uk. This is much easier and clearer to read and much more practical, not just on business cards and for emails but in this situation on property adverts and on 'For Sale' boards.

BUYING AND REGISTERING A DOMAIN NAME

There are literally hundreds of places online where you can buy a domain name, some more expensive than others. You should also be able to entrust your website designer to do this for you. Just remember to stipulate that the domain name must be registered in the company name or the 'managing director trading as' etc. It is not to be registered in their name under any circumstances; this is very bad practice, although unfortunately some website design agencies do this.

As already mentioned, .co.uk is the most common option used in the UK and these types of domain names are generally looked after by Nominet, one of the world's leading internet registry companies.

NOMINET

Ideally, when buying a .co.uk try to ensure that whoever you are buying it from (either directly or via the website designer) is a member of Nominet, as this means that they will follow their rules and guidelines. The team at Nominet basically manages all domain names that are part of the .uk top-level domain such as .co.uk, .org.uk, .gov.uk, .me.uk, etc.

Nominet's technical expertise helps them to manage the .uk domain space. It is a non-profit-making public purpose company with over 2,800 current members.

One of the best things about Nominet is its dispute resolution service. This is impartial and provides great assistance should the need arise with an issue relating to a domain name under their control. The team supports both registrars and registrants of domain names, hence using a member of Nominet to register your domain name is a sensible move.

The Nominet members' logo

SPECIFICALLY .CO.UK

Up until 2012, .co.uk domain names could only be registered for a two-year period at a time. However, in 2012 the rules changed, allowing people to register .co.uk, .org.uk, .me.uk domain names etc. for between one and ten years at a time. Naturally the longer you renew it for the more it will cost in the short term, but registering for longer does mean that you do not have to think about renewal for some considerable time. If you already have a domain name at the next renewal period, you will be asked if you want to renew it for up to a further nine years.

At the time of writing, you should expect to pay no more than £100 plus VAT for a ten-year term. Once registered a domain name is yours until renewal, and as the registrant you will be given the first opportunity to renew it. If for any reason you forget to action the renewal then you have a grace period of about ninety days before it becomes available to the general public for anyone to register in their name. You will get a number of reminders during this period, although in most cases your website design agency or website hosting provider will take care of this for you.

The correct registrant is critical!

Out of all the general information in this book, this is probably the most crucial bit. If you remember only one thing going forward, let it be this. This is one area where I have spent a lot of time over the years helping people out; it can be a very big problem for you and your business if you do not get it right.

I cannot stress enough how important it is when registering a domain to ensure that it is registered to the right person and business name. The following guidelines spell out what should be listed:

- If the domain name is for a Limited company then it MUST be registered to the Limited company.
- If you are a sole trader then it should be registered in the owner's name and 'trading as' and the business name.

- If the business is a partnership then it needs to be registered in the name of the partnership, not one of the partner's names.
- If you are a charity then – similar to a Limited company – the charity's name and number should be entered with the point of contact (the current chairperson). The contact name can always be changed but the registrant cannot.
- For other UK entities such as clubs and associations, the name of the club is the owner with the current chairperson/treasurer as point of contact.

WHEN DOMAIN NAME REGISTRATION GOES WRONG

The following are real stories and situations that I have been involved with over the last couple of years. Full disclosure of the real business and personal names has not been given. I have come up against a number of similar situations multiple times over the years.

'MY WEB DESIGNER TOLD ME NOT TO REGISTER IT IN MY REAL NAME'

This is the strangest one I have ever come across, and thankfully only the one time. My client had a small website that he used to help children in Africa get laptops. It was a personal charitable hobby, done in his spare time. The website had been set up by an independent website designer some time ago and the owner came to me through a recommendation as he had discovered that he was no longer getting any emails from the website.

The enquiries were from people offering him their old laptops which he could fix and send to Africa. He only found this out by chance when someone he knew asked him how things were going and they got talking. He explained that things had been quiet and that he was not getting many enquiries. It came to light that this person had sent an email not long ago and that his colleague had collected the laptop from him. The owner could no longer contact the website designer but had basically established that the same designer had been taking the email enquiries and subsequently the laptops.

I got involved as he called into my office and asked what, if anything, he could do, as the domain name was printed on a number of things and it would be costly to change, especially for a charitable hobby. We started some investigation and I discovered that it was not registered in his trading name, his personal name or even that of the website designer. It was in a random name, and he explained that he was told not to register it in his own name but to make one up. This meant that as no real person owned the domain name and the website designer was not contactable or likely to make a transfer to a new provider, my client was stuck.

After an hour's brainstorming and investigation we had a letter of confirmation from his accountant confirming that his bank had paid for the domain name. We submitted this to Nominet and, being very helpful as ever, they transferred the

IPS TAG to our servers (an IPS TAG – Internet Provider Security TAG – is the technical term that identifies the hosting company of a .co.uk or .org.uk domain name), so that we had control of the domain name if not the ownership. In the meantime one of my team downloaded the site files from the internet and re-uploaded them to our servers. Within twenty-four hours the site was back live with emails going to the right person.

This got things up and running and we are in control of the domain name and emails now, but the legal ownership is still in the name of a fictitious person and this cannot be changed. I just hope that no one of that name ever has a business use and wants it, or things could get a little tricky.

'MY WEB DESIGNER REGISTERED IT FOR ME AND HE HAS NOW EMIGRATED'

This particular issue came to light when the owners of the website wanted a new one. The original website designer had emigrated a few years back and when the owners visited me to see how we could help, it wasn't long before the subject of domain names came up. It turned out they had two, one used for emails and one for the website. As mentioned earlier, sometimes this can be a good thing. It was an overly compli-cated situation as the domain name used for the website was registered to, and therefore owned by, the emigrant website designer whom no one could contact. The one used for emails was owned by an IT company, which had told my clients they needed a second one as there was nothing that could be done about the first domain name. The original website designer had registered it in his name (probably in good faith, but still the wrong thing to do).

The IT company was accessible so it was easy for that domain name to be pointed to a new website, but first we had to get access to the website domain name so that once a new one was designed and built it could replace the one that everyone knew about and used. Again the cost of re-marketing and changing domain names on stationery and signage would have been very costly.

Fortunately, in this case the clients had kept all the emails from years ago, and by working through them we could prove that they had paid the (now emigrant) website designer for the domain name purchase. Armed with this, we could prove to Nominet that it was theirs and the transfer of ownership could be made into the right name. Note, however, that this did take some time; be aware it is not always something that can be sorted within twenty-four hours.

'MY WEB DESIGNER REGISTERED IT AND HAS GONE BUST AND NO ONE KNOWS WHERE HE IS'

This can be one of the worst-case scenarios. I have seen this happen on a number of occasions, usually with small start-up web design agencies or friends of the family that could design and build a website but have then moved away. It is very important to remember to make sure you pay for your own domain name and get an invoice for it in the company name.

On this occasion I had helped a client who had used a young man to design a website in a contra-deal situation. The young man knew how to design and build a website and said that he would create one for this mechanic in return for some car maintenance. He also registered the domain name and set up the email accounts, in his own name. All was done and dusted, car fixed and website live, so both parties got their end of the deal. The hosting suddenly stopped (probably as the contract had run out), so the website and the emails both stopped working. The young man had moved on and seemed to have disappeared. The mechanic could not get access to the domain name and on this occasion it wasn't good news. He had no proof of any ownership as it was handshake deal; the domain name was just a personal name and it was used on his van, adverts, stationery, marketing material and much more. In the end, we had no choice but to register a new one and we used a hyphenated version, but costs were still incurred in changing the marketing material.

'MY BOYFRIEND SORTED MY WEBSITE OUT AND WE HAVE SPLIT UP'

This is very similar to the previous example: a businesswoman set up a restaurant and her long-standing boyfriend helped her out with a number of things at the time, one of which was the website. He sorted out the design, the build and the hosting and registered the domain name online; and – more than likely without thinking – registered it in his name and not that of the business of which he was never officially part. When the relationship broke down a couple of years later, it wasn't particularly amicable and he had full control of the domain name and therefore the website and all email accounts. In this instance we managed to get the transfer made as we could prove that the domain name renewal over the previous years had been paid from the business bank account. Again this did take time to sort and my client was without a website and email for some time. No doubt the business will have lost some income from that downtime, but at least new signage wasn't required.

'MY PARTNER REGISTERED THE DOMAIN NAME; HE HAS NOW LEFT THE COMPANY – AND NOT ON GOOD TERMS'

This situation is much more common than you may think. As any solicitor will tell you when setting up a business, make sure that everything is written down and contracted when there is more than one person involved. Many people start businesses with very good friends or family and do not expect that anything will go wrong, but believe me, things *do* go wrong.

There was a situation where a company was set up by two people who had been very good friends for many years. Initially things went well and each one had their own part of the business to deal with. A few years in, however, things started to go wrong and they both blamed each other for it not going according to plan. One half left to set up on his own and the other carried on with the existing company. At the point of change, the owner who was left with the original company discovered that the domain name had been registered in his friend's own name, not that of the business. Not only had the two gone their separate ways in business but they were also no longer friends; and the one who left had not only decided to set up on his own doing the same thing, but also that he was going to use the original domain name as he owned it. In this case there was no Limited company set up to claim any rights to it; the person who registered the domain name paid for it out of his own pocket before they started trading, so there was no invoice in the company name. He had the right to use it and had a big advantage as the search engines liked the domain name because it had been used successfully for a number of years and had worked its way up the ranking. In this case there was nothing that my client could do other than register a different domain name. At the same time he took the opportunity to get rebranded, at some expense.

Remember

When registering a domain name it should be in the business name with the Managing Director, or CEO or owner as the person named. If it is a Limited company then the name 'trading as' should be registered along with the Limited company number. This means that should anything happen, as long as you can prove you are from the trading company then there is a much better chance that you will gain control of it and quickly, subject to any legal challenges from the other party.

The contact information is usually that of the website designer or hosting provider as they will sort out the renewal and any technical issues, but that can easily be changed at any point. The registrant cannot be changed; once it is registered that is who owns the domain, and unless they co-operate there is little that can be done to change it, other than by a legal challenge or, if it is a .uk domain, then via Nominet with proof.

CHECKING IF YOU OWN YOUR OWN DOMAIN NAME

This is much easier than you think. If you are not sure who owns a domain name it is always a good idea to check and then get it corrected while on good terms with whoever does.

There are a number of WHOIS options (WHOIS is the technical term for finding out who owns a domain name) but a quick one is to use Nominet (www.nominet.org.uk). Here you can click the 'whois' option and search for who owns any .co.uk or .org.uk domains; there is no registration and the information is freely available.

If you want to check a .com or .net then there are a number of easy-to-use options; the vast majority of variants can be seen here – the common one is whois.com. In some cases the owner can pay to OPT OUT of displaying their ownership. If you find out that that the owner has chosen to opt out (and this isn't you) then you need to do some more investigating to find out who registered it.

If you find that the domain name is not registered to the right name then you need to ask the person in whose name it is registered to change it. With any of the .uk extensions Nominet will charge a small administration fee of about £15. With dot.coms the person with access to the account can just change the name without incurring a fee. Trust me, it is well worth getting this corrected.

5
MEETING YOUR WEBSITE DESIGNER/DEVELOPER

This chapter is aimed primarily at business owners or marketing managers who are looking to use an outside website design agency for their web work. The questions are worded so that the designer/sales person will think that you know what you are talking about (even if you do not!). Be aware, too, that some website designers may give the impression that they can do anything; and whereas their designs frequently look amazing, they may not have the technical skills necessary to develop the site and make it work to its full potential. Check that your chosen website designer has the right experience and a proven successful track record.

This chapter also provides useful background information for those looking to recruit an in-house website designer/developer. Once again beware: a portfolio of design work may look good but it does not give any indication as to whether the website will work for you and for your customers. If you are armed with the right questions and have a rough idea of what answers to expect, potential candidates will not be able to baffle you with jargon and make out they are more experienced than they really are.

WILL MY WEBSITE BE BUILT IN A CONTENT MANAGEMENT SYSTEM?

This is very important as you want to have access to your website to make changes as and when required without incurring any extra cost, but more importantly in a time-frame that suits you and your business. You do not want to be in a position of emailing your website designer with changes or a news story and then finding that the update cannot be done for a few days due to other work commitments.

A content management system (CMS) is basically a user-friendly front-end system that you can login to once the website is built and make changes to content. In theory you can change much more but do remember that a website is built in code and is complex; start fiddling and you soon 'get in too deep' and end up in a mess. Most of the time having access to edit content, images, add news and update calendars is all that you will need.

Once logged in you should be able to make changes within minutes, much more quickly than emailing changes to your website designer.

It is always worth asking the website designer what content management system they use and why. If they have developed their own system this may cause problems if later you wanted to change provider or they go out of business. Another agency would then have to rebuild a new website from scratch. There are many very good content management systems available and all design agencies should be able to pick up a mainstream one and amend it if appropriate to do so.

It is also worth asking how user-friendly the system is; ask too if you can have a look at the back end. Some of the systems have built-in flexibility that is great for website designers but a nightmare for end users to understand; and if you are going to be updating your own website in-house it needs to be easy for you and your team to use. If a designer is reluctant to show you what they use or give you access to have a look, do question why. You are paying for your own website and going forward you need to know that it is the best thing for you and your business.

There are of course some cases where a complex website is required and general content management systems are not suitable for the job; in these instances a bespoke back-end system is developed for a specific project. For the vast majority of small businesses, however, this is not usually the case.

WHAT LANGUAGE WILL MY WEBSITE BE WRITTEN IN?

By this I mean the programming language. Any discussion about this area will involve the use of jargon, so this section introduces you to some of the more common terms used. Check that the website designer or design agency is using a language that is current, and not an older version. This ensures that they are building you a sustainable website and not one that is out of date in terms of technology before it even goes live.

There are a number of languages that can be used to build websites, and a basic understanding of these is useful (see also Appendix 1).

- **HTML5** At the time of writing this is the most current web language. Although it has been around since 2010/2011 it is not yet classed as officially standard, and is expected to become official in 2014. Make sure your chosen website designer uses this language.

- **XHTML** There are a number of versions of XHTML but all of them are older than HTML5, so ideally look for a website designer who has moved on. XHTML comes in two versions: transitional and strict. If the website is being built in this language then it should be tested to the strict level.

- **HTML4** This was developed in the late 1990s. Avoid any website designer still using this.

- **Flash** Many websites in the early part of the twenty-first century used this technology. It made websites look very sleek and sexy, and graphically anything could be done to make images move. In its day this was very impressive; however, as times have moved on, websites using Flash have encountered problems. Flash will not work on an iPhone or iPad unless the website designer also builds a non-Flash version – which begs the question, what is the point? Using Flash also means that you need to have a text-only version to ensure that it complies with the Equality Act and that a visually impaired person's screen reader can access the website (see Chapter 3). There is also a question over whether search engines can read all the information within a Flash file. For these reasons – and the fact that it would be designed in a way that would prevent you and your team from updating your website – avoid it. Nowadays, the vast majority – if not all – things that could be done in Flash can be done using Java Script.

- **PHP** This is not the language a designer writes in but something that a developer will develop the website in, and the two go hand in hand. It is one of the most commonly used languages, especially for websites that are active and 'talk' to different types of databases (an example could be an estate agent where the property data is stored and is searchable by the end user). This language is classed as 'open source'; it is the opposite of Microsoft and many developers can access the code and develop more things to work with it. Websites built using PHP can be hosted on either a Microsoft Windows or Linux server.

- **ASP/ASP.NET** This is a Microsoft product and is an alternative to PHP. Developers will choose one or the other depending on their training and personal preference. Once again this is suitable for an active website that talks to a database. A website built using this must be hosted on a Windows server, which is relevant if you are arranging your own website hosting.

WILL MY WEBSITE BE A BESPOKE DESIGN OR FROM A TEMPLATE?

Your website may be the first impression that someone gets of you and your business. If the end user accesses the internet on a regular basis and sees that your website uses the same layout as another but with different colours and a different logo what does that say about you? You and your business are unique; you offer products and services as do your competitors, but in order to win the work all small business owners have to offer added value. Your website needs to stand out from the crowd.

I do not like to use templates but I accept that they have their place. There are a number of small businesses local to me that have a template web page and it is noticeable as soon as you go there. To me this says: 'I need to be on the internet but I'm not really that bothered so what's the cheapest option?' That makes me think about the rest of their services: do they apply the same theory to any other areas? A cynical view, maybe, but I am not alone in thinking this.

A question of cost

Be aware that some website designers will charge the same price for a template as for a bespoke design. You may think using a template is the cheaper option but that is not necessarily the case. And remember: you and your business are unique, so should not your website be?

If you are going down the road of designing and building your own website then using one of the online 'build your own websites' is a good option. Here you will be able to choose from hundreds if not thousands of basic templates that you can personalize with your own colours, logos, images and content. A website designer, however, should not be using these; they should design and build one exclusively for you, from scratch, based on your existing branding.

If you are not sure of the website designer's usual practice have a look at their portfolio online. Do the websites look very similar (template) or are they very different (bespoke)?

WHAT TESTING WILL YOU DO ONCE MY SITE IS BUILT?

This question really tests the website designer's knowledge and expertise. The answers you should get include the answer to the next question about web browsers. Make sure, too, that the designer mentions the Equality Act and the EU Cookies Directive (see Chapter 3) and ideally the current web industry standards (see below).

WHAT BROWSERS WILL MY WEBSITE BE MADE TO WORK WITH?

This question is to ensure that the website designer is not cutting any corners and that they will check that the website will work for the majority of end users. All website designers will have a preferred website browser for their own personal use, and for many this will be Google Chrome. That is all well and good, but what do your customers use?

You need to ensure that your website designer tests the website in a number of website browsers and also different versions of those browsers.

The latest statistics[11] show that Chrome is the most popular browser, but just under three people in ten use different versions

---

11 http://www.sitepoint.com/browser-trends-may-2013/?utm_medium=email&utm_
campaign=DesignFestival+May+1st&utm_content=DesignFestival+May+1st+Version+
A+CID_4d967fe641441161aee5869a4e8da155&utm_source=Newsletter&utm_term=
Browser+Trends+May+2013+IE8+Drops+Below+10

of Internet Explorer, two in ten are using Firefox and many Apple users have Safari (including on an iPad). It is worth noting that versions 6 and 7 of Internet Explorer are not generally supported.

Worldwide Browser Statistics March 2013 to April 2013

The following table shows browser usage movements during the past month.

Browser	March	April	change	relative
IE (all)	29.29%	29.69%	+0.40%	+1.40%
IE10	2.26%	6.19%	+3.93%	+173.90%
IE 9	15.81%	13.35%	-2.46%	-15.60%
IE8	10.29%	9.30%	-0.99%	-9.60%
IE7	0.64%	0.59%	-0.05%	-7.80%
IE6	0.29%	0.26%	-0.03%	-10.30%
Chrome	38.13%	39.21%	+1.08%	+2.80%
Firefox	20.85%	20.05%	-0.80%	-3.80%
Safari	8.48%	7.99%	-0.49%	-5.80%
Opera	1.16%	1.00%	-0.16%	-13.80%
Others	2.09%	2.06%	-0.03%	-1.40%

Worldwide browser statistics March–April 2013

In addition to testing in multiple browsers, you should expect the website designer/agency to say that they will test to ensure compliance with the Equality Act (covered in much more detail in Chapter 3) and against the W3C standards to ensure there are as few technical code errors as possible.

DO YOU INCLUDE ANY SEARCH ENGINE OPTIMIZATION (SEO)?

Search engine optimization is covered in detail in Chapter 6. It is a very large subject that is constantly evolving, but I believe that the on-site basics should be included as standard. I am aware, however, that this is sometimes asking too much of smaller design agencies as they are primarily designers who cannot really be expected to keep up with the endless changes and developments.

By 'the basics', I mean:

- Adding the title tags to each page and not leaving them as 'Home' or the 'Company Name', for example.
- Making sure that all images, logos and graphics have descriptions.
- Each page should have a basic page description set up in the back end.
- Setting up each page with a friendly URL where possible.
- Using relevant headings within H1 and H2 tags.

If the website designer says that this is not included as it is not their area of expertise then you can do it yourself once you have access to the content management system.

CAN YOU DESIGN A MOBILE-FRIENDLY VERSION?

As mentioned in Chapter 2, as more and more people access the internet via their smartphones, having a mobile-friendly version of your website becomes all the more important. All good website designers should offer you this service at the same time as developing your main website in order to keep costs down.

Mobile website design can, however, be seen as a specialist area; ask to see examples of work to make sure that your web designer can deliver one, and check what will be included.

One important question at this stage is to ensure that both websites will be updated from the same place at the same time. You want to avoid having to update the main website's content in one system and then again in another.

Note that the website designer/agency may offer you a responsive website; one that responds to the size of the screen. Therefore it fits on a desktop, and if you make the window smaller it will reduce in size but keep functionality (down to the size of a smartphone screen). It is really just another way of saying that it is mobile-friendly.

WHERE WILL MY WEBSITE BE HOSTED?

I cover the subject of website hosting in more detail in Chapter 7, but it is good to find out where the web designer hosts their websites. Ideally, you want to ensure that your website will be hosted in the UK or the EU. You also want to know what, if any, restrictions are in place in terms of a limit to the amount of space on your website, or the bandwidth. Not having enough space, for example, can cause you an issue if you are uploading images. You want to ensure that your websites do not have to share server space with other companies.

CREATING YOUR BRIEF AND WORKING OUT WHAT YOU WANT

It is always great when a client comes to see me or my team and has a basic idea of what they want. It is not about the customer knowing the way the website should look – that is the designer's job and what they are getting paid for – it is more about what the customer wants on the website in terms of functionality and content. Any good website designer/developer can design and build anything: the usual restriction on design is budget. If you go into a meeting with no ideas at all, it can be hard to get going and much time will be spent on working out what will be on the website rather than on the look and feel. Some website design agencies may charge per meeting, so the more preparation you can do in advance the less it will cost you.

START WITH A SIMPLE BRIEF

Before you approach someone to design your website, prepare a list of page names and write a brief sentence describing what will be on each page. Here are some ideas on what you may want to think about for the general pages and sections of your website.

Home page

This is the first thing that most people will see.

- State what you do and where you do it.
- Do you want a news section? Will you have time to update it? There is nothing worse than seeing a news section with out-of-date news; people may question whether you are still trading. Updating news is great if you have something to say and the resources to update it on a regular basis.

- Do you have any videos that can be added? If you do then embedding them from YouTube is a great idea.
- Are you a Twitter or any other social media addict and, if so, do you want to have a feed on the home page? If you do, have you thought of the last tweet or more?
- Call to action – in most cases the purpose of your website is to gain more sales and enquiries, so what is your preferred method? It may simply be a telephone number; you may want to have a live chat feature, where the end user can type in a question on the web page and one of your team will get a notification and be able to reply immediately.
- Do you want or need to make use of large photographs here? A restaurant, for example, would have photos of their creations and the venue. These – and perhaps changing images – can be a far more effective sales tool than words alone.

Contact page

Most websites will have a contacts page, but it is not essential if, for example, you work from home where you may have a contact number and email only and no address or map is needed. If this is the case, the contact information is usually in the header.

- Do you want an enquiry form for people to complete, giving basic information such as name, email, telephone and subject box? Or do you want to include a drop-down list of services offered for the customer to refer to? Some people like forms, and others prefer simply to have an email address and telephone number. It comes down to personal preference.

- Have you a location where people visit? If so, a map is always a good idea; and if you do not have private parking provide information on the best place to park.
- If you do have visitors then your opening hours will probably need to go on this page too.
- Include full contact information for all locations if the company has more than one.
- If you are a Limited company you may use this page to add your company registration information.

Services

This section is usually the chunky element to a website as it details what you and your business offer.

- This page may be broken down further, for example a firm of solicitors will offer different areas of law, so this page may list subheadings which take the user to a fresh page for each, such as: Criminal Law; Family Law; Commercial Law.
- You may want to show a price list; for example, this is a common feature within the hair and beauty industry. The price list would have a page of its own.
- You may want to have a section that is only accessed once someone has subscribed, with specific downloads available.

Gallery

- Have you got things to show off? Tradespeople can show off 'before and after' images of their work. Equally a gallery is crucial for a photographer or an artisan.

Meet the team

- Do you want photos of each person with a small biography or would you prefer a team photo?
- Do you want to have a page for each person, or will one page for the company or main team suffice?

General content pages

- All websites have a number of general content pages and a list of these can be helpful so that the website designer can establish the size of the navigation they have to work with.
- Not all pages will be in the main navigation: some will be at the bottom, such as terms and conditions.

In addition to pages, all websites contain two very useful areas: the header and footer.

Header

The very top of the page.

- This is where your logo will be, in most cases to the left (but there is no rule attached to position).
- If you are active on social media websites then you may want to have the relevant icons here for people to like or follow.
- Do you send newsletters to your customers or potential customers? If you do, then you may want to encourage more people to sign up to receive it, in which case having the newsletter sign up in the header on all pages could be a good idea.

- Any call to action such as phone numbers and email addresses may be added here so that people do not have to search through the website pages to find such details.

Footer

At the bottom of each page.

- If you have affiliations to any organizations, do you want to show them and link to those websites? If so, do you want to display their logos?
- Company registration details could be here (if you are a Limited company this must be on your site somewhere).
- Again, to save people searching, do you want your address on all pages?
- The privacy policy, terms and conditions and sitemap links are usually here and the website designer will normally add any additional SEO key phrases to this area.

This may seem like a lot of work, but not every business will use all these elements. Compile a list of the pages that you feel you need. It is a good starting point and will help the process along, but it is not cast in stone.

DESIGN

Design is always a personal choice and what you may like is not necessarily the same as what someone else may like. Website designers are always happy to help and have great creative skills but they have to understand what you like to ensure that their design is close to what you want. If the web designer can get the look and feel right first time, it will help speed up the whole process.

If you have seen a couple of websites that you like (not necessarily in your industry) then show the designer. Equally, if you have seen one you really dislike, let them see this too. Although the website is always aimed at the end user, you have to be happy with it too. If you have no set ideas, knowing if you want clean and crisp or soft with colour is very helpful to the designer as they will get an idea of you and your personality.

At the initial brief/meeting the detail is not required, just an overview of what you are offering to your end users. Once the designer has this information it is then their job to go off and design a website that includes all the things you want but in a user-friendly way while keeping any existing corporate branding intact.

6
GETTING TO KNOW BASIC SEARCH ENGINE OPTIMIZATION (SEO)

SEARCH ENGINES

> A Web search engine is a tool designed to search for information on the World Wide Web. Information may consist of web pages, images, information and other types of files. Some search engines also mine data available in newsbooks, databases, or open directories. Unlike Web directories, which are maintained by human editors, search engines operate algorithmically or are a mixture of algorithmic and human input.

> Wikipedia

There are a number of search engines, some large, some small. The most commonly used are Google, Bing (formerly MSN.Live), Yahoo and YouTube. YouTube is owned by Google and accounts for a good number of results from searches. Video is playing a increasingly important role within search engine optimization and, when embedded into a website from YouTube, seems to give some advantage.

As the chart shows, Google is by far and away the most used search engine, so generally most SEO is done to their guidelines.

The key is to remember that the website is, first and foremost, for the end user. In order for Google to be the best search engine it must give its end users the best set of results that it possibly can.

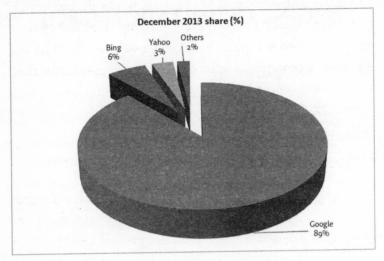

The market share of search engines[12]

WHAT IS SEARCH ENGINE OPTIMIZATION?

Put simply this is a method of getting a website to appear as high up as you can in search engines such as Google, Bing and Yahoo. Every company wants their business to be at the top of page one but we all know that only one website can be number one for each search term that someone has entered. The last part of that statement is of key importance; you may be number one on page one for one search term, but a slight

---

12 http://theeword.co.uk/info/search_engine_market.html

variation may place you somewhere else. This may still be on page one, or lower down the rankings on a later page.

I do not profess to be an SEO expert, but as the owner of a web design agency it is important that my team and I know the basics when it comes to building a website. We work on the basic webmaster guidelines that Google provides for free, and as they update and alter their guidelines we try to adapt accordingly.

SEARCH TERMS

A search term is what someone enters into their chosen search engine to find services, companies or general information. Individuals will word things differently even though they may be looking for the same answer. As an example, some may search for 'a Chinese takeaway in Anytown' and another may enter 'Anytown takeaways'. If you own a Chinese takeaway then your website will come higher up the rankings with the first search term than the second. Compensating for all variants is where the time and skill comes in to SEO.

AREAS OF SEARCH ENGINE OPTIMIZATION

SEO is usually split between on-site and off-site optimization. The following list covers a few of the main areas:

- **Basics on the website (on-site)** I will cover this area later in this chapter in more detail.

- **Social media integration** As more and more people use social media websites such as Twitter and Facebook, linking from these sites in posts to your website can help improve your position in the search engine rankings.

- **Pay per click (PPC)** When you do a search on Google you will see adverts in the right-hand column and in a shaded area at the top of the page. These are paid-for adverts; the more people who click, the more it will cost you to advertise on that page. The cost can vary enormously from a few pence to hundreds of pounds if you are in a high-value industry with lots of competition. The more you are prepared to pay when someone clicks the link, the higher up in those lists you will be.

- **Link building** This is not as popular as it once was as the search engines have reduced its importance, but it is still of some relevance. It is basically finding websites that are relevant to your business and having a link on their website back to your own. For example, if you are a chartered surveyor or accountant and part of a recognized institution, linking other members' websites back to yours would help.

- **Google Adwords** This is intelligent marketing where you place an advert and then it follows anyone who has searched for anything similar on any website adverts. Charges are based on the number of times the advert is shown and clicked on.

GETTING TO GRIPS WITH SEO

Clients have said to me that SEO is something of a 'black art' to them but once the basics have been explained they are less wary of it. When you manage your own content on your website and your blog, you need to understand the importance of the links, the friendly URLs and the title tags.

Your website is just one part of your marketing strategy, but your clients may get to see it via a number of different routes: through networking and handing out business cards with the site address on, or responding to an advertisement on the side of a vehicle or building signage. It may be that someone is searching for the services you offer online, and this is where SEO comes in. My company gets most of its work through word of mouth and recommendations, not via our website. The website does have the basic SEO running through it, and we have some links from other sites (including those we have designed) but we do not spend money on 'pay per click'.

> **TIP** SEO may or may not play an important part in your marketing strategy; just remember it exists. Doing the basics will do no harm and can only help.

HOW DOES GOOGLE WORK?

Google doesn't tell anyone how it places websites but it does give quite a lot of guidelines and hints. It also changes its algorithms on a regular basis to prevent any spammers trying to fool its systems and get rubbish websites to the top.

As mentioned earlier, Google wants to be the best in its own field and as such wants to give the end user the best set of results it can; so if I search for a painter in my local town then I expect to get a list of painters in my local town, not in London for example. For Google to do this, however, it needs to know which painters are there. It looks at a number of aspects including Google Places (see page 103), as well as reading all the text information on a website and placing relative importance on the content.

CONTENT IS KING

For the search engines to find your website you must have plenty of good, well-written relevant content for them to read. If you are a travel agent, for example, and the content doesn't mention the words 'travel agents' (and just talks about the holidays that you have on offer), how can Google find you when someone searches for a travel agent? It is not likely to bring your website back in its results as it doesn't know that you are a travel agent unless you tell it. Exceptions to this rule are the bigger companies; as they are so well known and have so much traffic, they do not need to place the same emphasis on content as a smaller business.

As a small business owner think very carefully about what you do and where you do it. Many businesses will say they will service anyone, anywhere, but this is not helpful when it comes to SEO. You need to think about the people who are searching for your services and include the words they use in the content. This refers back to the search terms; it is a bit like playing snap in that Google searches for matches. Having the phrase that someone is most likely to enter into Google within your content is a great starting point.

People are not likely to search for 'welcome', 'home' or 'established since 1066', so do not place those words and phrases at the top of pages and in key places such as the headings or subheadings. Using the travel agent as an example, the heading could say 'ABC Travel Agents of ABC Town'. If someone searched for that (a strong possibility), there is a higher chance of finding it.

Where those key phrases are placed is very important as they signal to Google the most important and the most relevant information that you want to get across.

HEADING TAGS

A heading tag is what the World Wide Web and SEO use in the same way that newspapers use headlines and subheadings: to highlight the most important bit of the story or content to the end user and grab their attention. With SEO you are trying to grab Google's and Bing's attention. Headings and subheadings in the online world are defined behind the scenes in the code/content management system via H1 to H6 tags: H1 being the headline and H2–H6 being subheadings. Using the heading tags is quite simple. If you are using a content management system you will have an online word editor and it should give you an option to highlight the headline and set a heading option. If you are using HTML then it will look similar to <h1>This is the heading</h1>

In the example below, both H1 and H2 headings have been used. The top headline 'Amanda J MacDougall, Burnley Accountant' is the H1, and the 'Welcome to AM Accounts Ltd, Accountants, Burnley' is the H2. These cover who she is, what she does and where, in a prominent place.

Screenshot identifying headings

Highlighting relevant keywords or key phrases in headings tells the world and the search engines that this is important information. The remaining content on that page gives more detail of what is on offer, and repeating keywords and phrases such as 'accountant(s)' and 'Burnley' backs up the importance of the headings. The majority of the world's population reads from left to right and top to bottom, and the guideline is that search engines work the same way; also that the headings for the first paragraph should be treated as more important than the last. The search engines have a lot to read very quickly so it is good practice to have relevant information higher up the page.

DOES SIZE MATTER?

As content is king, the more relevant content that you have on your website the better, but the keyword here is 'relevant'. Obviously if you try and get everything that your business offers onto one or two pages with a view that the smaller the website is, the less it will cost you to build, you will be correct. However, having just two pages and cramming everything onto those is unwise as the search engines will have fewer pages to read and the end user may have to scroll through masses of other website details in order to find you. This could result in spending money on something that will not work.

Equally, too many pages can put people off, especially if the content is simply repeated. When you land at a website you know what you are looking for so reducing the number of clicks to get to that information is important. If you have multiple navigations to click through, for example one at the top and then another down the side, you will soon get bored.

There is no golden rule on how many web pages you should have, and the more services you offer the larger the website will be. If you only have a small selection of services you may want to have a page for each, and one page with a couple of paragraphs for those that can be combined. Only you know your business and the areas that you want your website to focus on. Which areas are the most profitable for you? What do you want to promote on the website? For more details on selecting suitable website pages, see Chapter 5.

On average most of my small business customers have between five and twelve pages of content on their websites.

FRIENDLY URLS

This is an easy-to-read link at the top of the page rather than one with lots of characters or irrelevant numbers.

- **Friendly URL** For example http://www.webdesign-issl.co.uk/website-design-examples.html is clearly written and easy for Google and other search engines to read.
- **Unfriendly URL** Along the lines of http://www.webdesign-issl.co.uk/blog/posts.aspx?id=999 where there is a question mark and page numbers within the link.

By default some content management systems automatically create a name for each page at the top (not the name within the navigation bar but in the actual link in the web browser address bar). The vast majority of content management systems allow the use of friendly URLS and there is usually a separate box on each page allowing you to enter the chosen information. If in doubt ask your designer, or if building your own website search the help pages for 'where to set a friendly URL'.

The friendly option can be read by search engines and gives the end user more chance of finding it if it matches the phrase they are looking for. In addition the friendly version says much more about the website than the unfriendly one.

TIP If you have a domain name that is your company name then making full use of friendly URLs is a really useful tool.

A good example of this is an estate agent with the company name Farrow and Farrow and the domain name Farrowfarrow.co.uk. This domain does not give much help with regard to SEO so introducing friendly URLs into the equation can help improve this. For example:

http://www.farrowfarrow.co.uk/rossendale-estate-agent.html is the link on the selling page, while http://www.farrowfarrow.co.uk/rossendale-letting-agent.html is the link for the letting page.

This can give an added enhancement to the SEO as you are giving the search engines something relevant to read right at the beginning. There is of course no surefire way of being on page one – let alone number one – but all these small steps can help (and cost nothing).

META ELEMENTS

Meta elements are the HTML or XHTML <meta> element used to provide structured metadata about a Web page. Multiple Meta elements with different attributes are often used on the same page. Meta elements can be used to specify page description, keywords and any other metadata not provided through the other head elements and attributes.

Wikipedia

Above is the technical definition of meta elements. Most people who have spoken to anyone or read anything about SEO will at some point have heard the term 'keywords'; and many people do get hung up on the term 'meta keywords' within the back end of a website. If you fall into this category then let me reassure you: Google has not used meta keywords for a few years and it is highly doubtful that any other of the big search engines do either.

In the past the keywords were used by search engines and did play a very important part. However, the search engines realized that this tool simply meant that anyone could spam the fields with keywords, key phrases and competitors' names in an attempt to be found when someone was searching for them. It wasn't long before Google and friends got wise and stopped using them. People still try to get around the measures in place to stop spammers and that is why the rules are constantly changing. One thing that remains true is: build the website for the end user first and foremost within the guidelines given and you will not go far wrong.

TITLE TAGS

A title tag is what is given to each page and is displayed when you hover over the tab in your browser on a web page. This is one of the first things that search engines can read so it is worth spending time putting some thought into this.

Using the example a local estate agent, the domain name is http://www.anthonyjturner.co.uk/ and the title tag of the home page is:

Estate | Estate Letting Agents Hebden Bridge Todmorden | Anthony J Turner

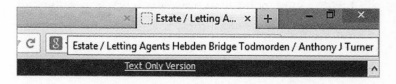

The title tag shown in the browser of the home page

The above example is on Anthony J Turner's website and is the home page title. It is what you can see when you hover over the tab. If you Google 'Hebden Bridge Letting Agents', you will see that this agent is the first true listing at the top (at the time of writing).

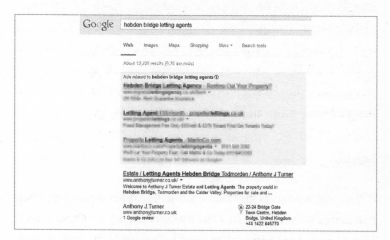

Screenshot of the Google search results

As this book is printed in black and white you cannot really tell, but links can show as different colours. The purple indicates that the link has been clicked on, but as you can see the top line shows the title tag after the company name with bold on the keywords between what was searched for and what was found. Google is intelligent when it comes to searching and giving back results.

Title tag length and content

The general guideline from major SEO experts (not Google) is that Google looks at approximately just sixty characters of text. This is one of the first areas that Google looks at (maybe after the domain name), so each page of a website should make full use of it. The phrase(s) here should be the most relevant to that page's content (note this is not your business name, unless it happens to be one and the same). If someone knows you they will find you using your name, not a search term. As we are not sure exactly how many characters are read, start with the most important information. Writing within sixty characters is more challenging than a Twitter post (it is less than half!). On the main website think about the page content, look at the heading and try to avoid having titles that cover everything you do. One key point to note is that all title tags need to be unique, so ensure that none are repeated.

If you have a page on a specific service then make sure that the title, the headings and the content all say what that page is about, i.e. that service. It should also cover where you offer it; someone looking for a letting agent may very well Google 'letting agent in Anytown' just as in my earlier example, so you need to make sure the town or area is in the title, the heading and if possible the URL. Below is another example from the Anthony J Turner website; this one is on the letting page and, as you can see, is different from the one on the home page shown on page 99.

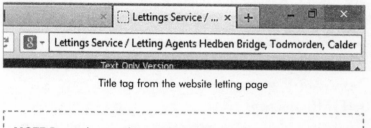

Title tag from the website letting page

NOTE Remember you have a title tag for each page.

The idea is to get the friendly URL, the title tag and the H1 tag to be the main (and the same) phrase you wish your page to be found under. This shows importance and relevance to both the end user and the search engines. It is not always possible as you still need to write the headings in good English, whereas the title and URL can ignore grammar and punctuation to reduce wastage of characters.

SITEMAP

There are two types of sitemap, both very similar, but one is specifically for Google and the other search engines and the other is for the end user. Simply put, a sitemap is a list of the pages that the site contains, a little like the final version of the original brief.

- **Sitemap.xml** This is for the search engines and is generated by the web designer once the website is built. There are lots of tools online that will help generate an xml sitemap and it is usually included in content management systems. Once you have created one you then submit it to Google, Bing and Yahoo etc. to help them crawl your website in a more efficient way. This is a direct way of telling them what pages you have.
- **HTML sitemaps** This is the human version, on the website; usually in the footer there will be a link to a page called sitemap. This will simply list the pages of content and may give a one-line text of what is there; each of the names will have a link to the actual page. This is very useful if you have a large website.

BREADCRUMBS

On some larger websites you may see a mini-navigation appear towards the top of the page basically showing you where you are. This allows you to move backwards and forwards without going back to the main navigation. It is very similar to navigating on a Windows computer when you drill down into folders and then go up a level when you cannot find what you are looking for without starting over.

The navigation underneath the main menu in the example is a breadcrumb trail and the end user can easily click back a section if required. This is a very good idea if you offer training guides or have a general information website rather than selling services. It is very similar to what you will see on e-commerce shopping sites.

Example of a breadcrumb trail

ALT ATTRIBUTE (ALT TAG)

This is an important attribute and is very easy to implement but so often ignored. It simply stands for alternate text and is relevant to all images, logos and graphics on a website. It is the text that goes behind any image to describe what it is: a photo, a picture or simply the company logo.

This is important for two reasons, the first being the Equality Act (see Chapter 3) and the fact that a blind person using a screen reader needs to have images read back to them so that they know what is being shown. The second is that Google and search engines are in effect 'blind'; they cannot interpret a picture unless there are words behind it saying what it is. If any relevant image or graphic is used then ensure that the alt attribute is used to describe it.

GOOGLE PLACES

This is not strictly search engine optimization but I think it needs to be mentioned and explained. At the end of the day, if you can get your business on page one of Google through having a Google Place, that can only be a good thing.

When you use Google as a search engine and you look for a business within an area, there is a good probability that towards the top of the results are lots of businesses with place markers next to them.

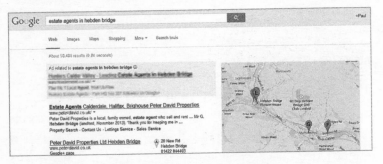

Screenshot of a Google search result

This example continues with the estate and letting agents in Hebden and you can see that I have copied the top two places. If you click on a place link you do not go direct to the website but you do get more information appearing to the right, as shown on page 105.

In order to get a Google Place, the first thing to do is search and see if there is one already there. If there is you can click through and claim it to be your own. When this originally started, Google gathered some of the data from sources such as *Thomson Local* and *Yell*, so the basics of the address were obtained along with a telephone number but not much else.

If on the other hand you cannot find one for your business, or you are a new business, then you need to create a Google account or sign in if you already have one. Once you are logged in, simply search for Google Places or go to http://www.google.co.uk/business/placesforbusiness and follow the prompts to create one.

Google Place example for Anthony J Turner

Whether you claim an existing place or create a new one, you will need to verify the account and you will either be given the option to verify by telephone or it will be by postcard. If the latter then expect a card with a code within twenty-one days; once you have submitted the code online it can take another fourteen days to be processed. The telephone option is the best as long as you do not have an automated message on your system, as it cannot deal with pressing 1, 2 etc, and will fail.

When your Google Place is set it up you can add photos, videos and of course a link to your website, in addition to the usual contact information and opening hours. Do make full use of the place as it can be a good way of getting more visitors to your website and possibly getting onto page one of Google.

Do take note, though, that this is not a quick process and you will not just knock someone off the page once yours is approved. Some suggest that a way to get higher up within the places listings is to get reviews via the review section within Google Places and other independent review sites.

SOCIAL MEDIA INTEGRATION

Over the last couple of years, social media integration has started to play a more important role within Google's ranking's algorithms, and as such probably the other search engines also.

Social media is its own specialist area and there are many experts out there. Giving your business a social media presence is without doubt a very important element of your marketing plan. When it comes to SEO, the more people who link to your website from Twitter, Facebook and LinkedIn (not forgetting YouTube), the more it can help. Much has been said over the years about link building but this is less important these days simply because the system was abused, with many links being generated from irrelevant and poor-quality websites.

However, if you are active on social media sites and are regularly posting and engaging with members of the public and others within your industry, then having them click through and visit your own website directly is a good thing. Google and no doubt the other search engines will place more relevance and importance on what you have to say and the articles, posts or pages that you are directing people to.

Having a page or an account and getting lots of likes and followers is a pointless exercise if you do not engage with them and direct them to your website. The idea is to use those websites to announce new products or services and to chat to anyone who is looking for what you do. Do remember, though, that you need them to click through in order to influence the optimization of the main website.

You can of course embed any of the social media feeds into your website and this is a great way of keeping your content fresh and up to date. It also means that you only have to update one thing, thus saving you time. There is, however, little point having both Facebook and Twitter feeds if they are going to show the same information in different detail. Choose the one you prefer and tie the two together but only show one on the website. Note that these feeds can slow down your website which can be a problem, especially as more and more people use wireless and 3G connections: they do not and will not wait for websites to load (see page 108). Do ensure that the person charged with embedding a feed does so in the most efficient way to help prevent any slowing down of your website, as this too can affect your website ranking.

BLOGGING

This is a good way of getting people involved with what you have to say and to show off your expertise, the key being getting people to look at your website. Many content management systems will have a blogging module and WordPress was created for blogging. Another option is to use Blogger, which is a Google tool, and have your website pick up the feed from it. With blogging you give each post a title and allocate keywords and phrases to it. Do remember, however, that blogging takes time and needs to be kept current; there is nothing worse than seeing out-of-date information on a website.

SPEED OF WEBSITE LOADING

The length of time it takes for a website to load can have an effect on the page rank that Google gives a website. As more people use WiFi and 3G/4G to access websites, one that is slow to load is at a disadvantage. There are a number of reasons why websites may be slow to load:

- **Image size** The size of the images being used. I have seen some large organizations and companies use very large images (each one 1.5MB, for example), even on the home page. There is no need for this as images for the internet can be optimized by using any number of free tools, and do not need to have the same high resolution as printed media. Reducing the size for online use will not reduce the quality or the detail, just the file size, and will therefore improve the time it takes for a web page to load. One tool to try is JPEGMini, which is designed to resize images without loss of quality.

- **Choice of server** This is covered in Chapter 7, but if the package that you or your website designer is using is not very good or has restrictions on the bandwidth usage, then this will have an impact on the loading time. This is generally the only expense you have once your website is designed and built, and if something is very cheap there may be a good reason behind it. Hosting should be within the UK, EU or a safe harbour such as the USA, simply because as a business owner you are responsible for the data. If you collect names and addresses for marketing/ newsletters or shopping then under data protection regulations you have a duty to protect that data. Check with your provider if you have any limitations that would impact speed either with your own site or the server as a whole.

- **Twitter feeds** An embedded Twitter feed has code to check and then update as and when necessary. Needless to say that this takes time and if Twitter usage is up for any reason, i.e. something very popular is trending, then their servers slow down and it takes longer for your element to get its information onto your web page. There are some helpful tips on the worldwide web that your website designer may be aware of, so it is worth asking for advice.

- **The 'little things'** There are a number of little things that can also add up when it comes to the time it takes for your web page to load, such as: advert choices, poor coding, multiple header and footer style sheets. This comes down to the standard that your website designer works to. Ensuring that you choose an experienced designer who uses current code and guidelines should help with these areas. As ever, lots of little things can add up to create bigger issues.

Think about loading time

The time it takes to load your website is so important, yet it is not really covered in great detail on a day-to-day basis. If a website is slow then the end user will get very frustrated and simply click the back button and look elsewhere. You may have very good broadband at the office but if your customers are finding you from their home, think about their broadband speeds and how long it may take for them to see the site. Chances are they are not on business broadband, and are using basic home WiFi routers, or 3G/4G.

TESTING THE SPEED OF YOUR WEBSITE

With the web browser Chrome you can run a test on your website and see how long it takes to load, and find out what it does once someone has entered the website address. It should not take very long and will put into perspective what I have been talking about.

1　Load up your website in Google Chrome.
2　Right click the page and select Inspect element; this will open a box at the bottom.
3　Choose the network tab (the third one along).
4　Back in the top half, where your website is showing, press CTRL, Shift and R on your keyboard.

5   Watch the files load and when finished have a look at the bottom to see how long it takes.

The information given is quite easy to interpret once it has finished loading. It will show you other information such as:

- **The number of requests that have been made** If your website is slow then looking at how many requests are being made will give you (or your website designer) an idea if it is loading too many different things, some of which may not be necessary.

- **A data transfer figure** This shows how much data was transferred; the higher the number the slower the site will be to load.

- **Load time** This will show you, hopefully in seconds, how long it took to load. If it shows you in minutes then either you have a very large website or something is making it very slow, in which case it needs to be looked into further.

The speed element of a website also backs up the need for a mobile-friendly website as they are specifically designed to work on a small screen and with a mobile connection.

> **NOTE** There are two load times: the 'onload' one is the time it takes for the initial content to load, whereas the general one is for the entire website to load.

The following screenshots are taken from www.issl.co.uk, a small business website. The first is the kind of screen you

should see when you run the test, and the second highlights
the key information that is displayed at the bottom.

Screenshot of what Chrome shows on a load speed test

49 requests | 89.2 KB transferred | 3.05 s (load: 3.06 s, DOMContentLoaded: 1.95 s)

Close-up information of the number of requests made and the time taken

The next one shows the same information but for the website
www.bbc.co.uk. As you can see, much more information is
being called – the requests being 100, and the amount of data
asked for much higher – yet the time it takes to load is very
short. This website, as you would expect, is very well built,
with the end user in mind.

103 requests | 608 KB transferred | 4.72 s (load: 2.80 s, DOMContentLoaded: 1.97 s)

Close-up of the speed test on the BBC website

This next one is from foxnews.com and accessed from the
UK. As you can see more than double the requests are being
made, but the time to load is longer.

235 requests | 1.1 MB transferred | 12.45 s (load: 11.18 s, DOMContentLoaded: 4.61 s)

Close-up of the speed test on the Fox News website accessed from the UK

NOTE To test your own website you need to clear your cache first, otherwise the true speed is not being shown. You can do this from within Chrome in the same Inspect element. Click on the Resources tab and under the heading Cookies, click on each one; where anything appears on the right click the item and press delete. Do this for all items, then click back to Network and refresh the page; this will give you a much more accurate picture from the perspective of a new end user who has not been to your website before.

GOOGLE ANALYTICS

This is probably the most well-known system for tracking visitors to your website. There are others that come with your control panel for the domain (also known as cPanel). If you use Google Analytics then there is a good chance you will need to have a privacy policy and have a 'We use cookies' pop-up linking to it. Some of the others do not use cookies but can still collect the data. Whichever system you look to use, there is a massive amount of data available.

This data shows you who is using your website in great detail, and includes such things as:

• Where the users are from (which country).
• What web browser they are using (Chrome, IE, Firefox etc.) and what version.
• What screen size they are using (800 x 600 pixels or wide screen etc.).

- Importantly, what pages of the website they look at: just the home page or any other in particular?
- How long they spend on the website: are they looking around or leaving as soon as they see the home page?
- The bounce rate – the lower the number the better. This is simply when someone goes to your website from a search engine and then straightaway clicks the back button in their browser. They may have clicked on your website link and then found it was not what they were looking for; or it could be that they found the site too fussy, did not know where to click next for what they wanted, so gave up and went back.
- The days and times that the website is busiest: Tuesday is usually slightly busier for some websites. This could be due to people using the internet in work time; Mondays are too busy to browse, but Tuesday is a little quieter with people having caught up with emails and messages from the weekend.

WHY IS THIS USEFUL?

If you know when your website is at its busiest, for example, you could post an offer on that day to get the most from it. Equally you could use that day to post one that is redeemable on a quieter day in the future, or to launch a new product or service.

If you see that the bounce rate is quite high (anything over 50 per cent should be looked at), it could be that the navigation isn't clear for the end user or the home page is taking too long to load.

Browser information is useful from a design and development perspective. If more and more people are using

Google Chrome over Internet Explorer, you need to ensure that your website works in that browser.

Knowing which pages people look at is crucial to your overall marketing. If you can see that some pages are getting fewer visitors than you would like, it may be that the page is not easily accessible. Maybe it is accessed only through a second site navigation and not the main one which is causing users not to see it (second navigations should be used with caution as they are not very user-friendly, but do have their place). Equally the time spent on the pages gives you a great idea as to what your potential customers are reading and what they like (and what they do not).

Track the website usage over time: is it getting more users or less? Naturally you want the user numbers to increase – taking into account any seasonal adjustments – and as long as this is happening then you are probably seeing the results in increased enquiries and therefore sales.

The following example is not from Google Analytics but a free control panel statistics monitor. In this case it shows a large jump in September from August 2013, so the question is: what marketing was done to generate this?

Visitors per Month			
11 Aug 2013 - 19 Jan 2014			
Date	Unique Visitors	Pageviews	Pages per User
August 2013	41,913	594,370	21.67
September 2013	98,698	1,562,525	19.60
October 2013	51,807	669,265	12.92
November 2013	49,467	1,199,159	24.24
December 2013	58,932	523,795	8.89
January 2014	25,121	185,690	7.39
		4,734,804	15.78

Some website user statistics

The example below shows the days that the website is used; Fridays are just about leading the way.

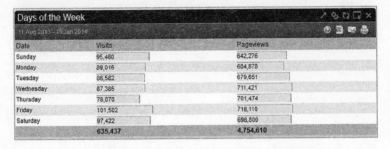

Date	Visits	Pageviews
Sunday	95,460	642,276
Monday	89,016	604,878
Tuesday	86,582	679,651
Wednesday	87,385	711,421
Thursday	78,070	701,474
Friday	101,502	716,110
Saturday	97,422	698,800
	635,437	4,754,610

Days of the Week — 11 Aug 2013 – 15 Jan 2014

Example of data per day to see which is the most popular

7
UNDERSTANDING HOSTING

Hosting plays an important part in your online presence. All websites have to be hosted on a server somewhere that has access to the worldwide web. This is not something that you can do yourself but there are many options available. In the vast majority of cases, however, you will not have any choice unless you are creating your own website. The website designer/design agency will already have their preferred hosting solutions for their clients, but it is important that you know what this actually includes.

IS THE SERVER SHARED WITH ANYONE ELSE?

Unless you use a large website design agency your designer is not likely to have their own dedicated server in a data centre, and to be honest there is no need. The important thing to know is whether the server hosting your website is being used by not just your web designer/design agency but by others. The cheapest option for designers is to rent a space on a shared server and to upload websites to it. The problem with this can be that they have a restricted amount of space and also a restricted amount of bandwidth (see page 119) that their clients can use.

Another important issue to think of with shared hosting is who else is on that server and what do their websites offer?

Website reputation matters with the search engines; if your website is hosted with lots of poorly built websites or those that are 'spammy' or sites with explicit content, it may seem suspicious and may affect your site. It is always a good idea to ask the designer where the site will be hosted and what others sites will be on there.

Some hosting providers will offer you SEO-friendly hosting; all this really means is that you will have your own IP address that only your website will be on. This gets round the issue of sharing with any spammy site but will cost you more. You will also need your own private IP (internet protocol) if your website uses SSL (secure sockets layer) for taking any online payments.

LIMITED SPACE

If using a shared account there may be times when your website is slow, or you may be restricted to the size of images that can be uploaded due to a limit on space. The latter was a problem I encountered with a local dance school; they had a website and access to the CMS, but when they went to upload new photographs they could not. Eventually they discovered that this was due to having exceeded the amount of space that they had been given.

As with most things you get what you pay for. The difference here is that unless you ask the question of your designer, you will not know what they have paid for on your behalf.

WHY BANDWIDTH IS IMPORTANT

Bandwidth is a measurement of data that is available and being used over a period of time. The hosting options your website designer has will determine how much your own website can use. In most cases this is not an issue but if you have a site that has a lot of images (for example, a photography business), having insufficient bandwidth can be a problem as your images may not be loaded.

Can your business cope if your website and emails go down?

Servers will go down at some point; at the end of the day they are all big computers with lots of elements that can simply stop working at any point. We have all had an experience where something just stops working and that is the end of its lifespan. However, with servers the key is to have options in place that reduce this risk to a minimum. Most servers will have multiple drives so that if one fails another will take over, but ask your designer about this as they may not have control over their own servers. If that is the case and they are sharing then your website may be down for some time, as could your email.

Downtime can also affect your SEO as down websites can lose their rank; and, if your site is down for a while, how will the search engines know about it or its content?

KNOWING WHERE YOUR WEBSITE AND DATA IS STORED

It is increasingly critical that as a business owner you know where your data is stored. Legal requirements under the Data Protection Act mean that you are responsible for that data. As long as the server is in the EU or a safe harbour such as the USA, then it should be protected under those rules. However, if your server is in a cheap hosting country you have no protection. If anyone accesses that server and uses any of your data, you are responsible.

There is also a chance that having your website hosted outside the country where your target market is (i.e. England) your search engine rankings will be affected. If you are in England and looking for a service, the search engines know where you are and where the website is hosted; logically, if the two are located in the same country this is beneficial. As with everything in the world of SEO, this is always changing and the effect may be small but nevertheless well worth mentioning.

IS YOUR DATA SECURE?

There are regular reports in the media about websites getting hacked (even very large organizations with no doubt top-class security systems, but the best hackers still manage to get in). In the real world of normal business your website can get hacked. This is not likely in order to bring you down on a personal level, but more likely because someone can. People write very clever computer programs that basically scour the worldwide web looking for 'open doors'; they enter in and either change the website or use any free space to store their own data. It seems that some people find this fun.

On a more serious level though, if you hold data within your website – for example, shoppers' details if you are selling online – then you are responsible for that. Some cheap and free hosting companies in parts of the world that are not classed as 'safe' may sell that customer data for their own financial benefit.

TIP Ask your designer where the site will be hosted, and with what else. You can use websites like www.whereisip.net to enter the IP address of the server and find out its location. Your web designer will have the IP address.

8
'THIS SITE MAY HARM
YOUR COMPUTER'

These words can strike fear and panic into any small business owner should they appear on Google search results under their web address. Fortunately I do not get involved with this sort of thing very often, but on one occasion I was asked to help a business associate who asked me to have a look at her website, as her clients were being warned to stay away. It is usually a friendly existing customer that brings this situation to your attention as it is very rare for a business owner to search for their own website.

REAL-LIFE CASE STUDY

This happened in July 2013 and at the time of writing is the most recent case I have been involved with. I received quite a frantic call from a known business associate explaining that this message was appearing when someone tried to access their website. They had logged into their CMS to see if they could work out what was wrong, but to no avail.

I did a search for the company name and, lo and behold, within Google results under the domain name it did say 'This site may harm your computer'. Having this message standing out clearly is never good for any business as it will prevent people from accessing the site. Anyone who does access it and who, for whatever reason, doesn't have any antivirus on their computer (never recommended) will more than likely have some malware or a virus downloaded to their computer.

I did click the link and, as expected, my very good antivirus kicked into touch the virus that tried to access my computer. This did make me wonder how many other people actually try these things? My associate was in a bit of a panic as this had been the case for a couple of days. One of her team had tried to sort out the problem on the WordPress back end but had not managed to get very far, and she was naturally concerned that she could be losing business.

HOW DID THE MALWARE/VIRUS GET IN?

The downside of using open-source content management systems such as WordPress is that they offer so much in the way of flexibility and plug-ins. (A plug-in is simply an additional tool that has been developed by someone working with the CMS, such as a calendar or news module.) Any one of those plug-ins may be vulnerable and allow a 'back door' to open. This basically means that when someone with too much time on their hands decides to write some code and send it off to infect a website, it goes looking for these open back doors and sneaks in. In this case there were a couple of back doors open through some of the pre-installed add-ons that came with the chosen template.

FEAR NOT, IT CAN BE FIXED... EVENTUALLY

Most things can be fixed – but you need to know how. In this particular case there were a couple of things that we had to do. First we accessed the WordPress content management system and found a number of things that should not have been there and got rid of them. Most of these revolved around the comments section of the website, which was open to allow end users to comment on articles and blogs that the business owner posted. At this point we only had access to the CMS and not the actual files so we were not sure if all doors were now locked. We proceeded to clean up the site and remove the infections that could be seen, and resubmitted it to Google. Overnight all was well again and the site was back to normal, but we did advise our client to change hosting.

The initial work got a temporary solution underway but during the investigation process we looked into the hosting of the website, and discovered that the server hosted a number of websites that were reported as having 'served content that resulted in malicious software being downloaded and installed without user consent'. It can be quite normal to have some on a server, but in this case over 65 per cent of the websites had an issue. This again stresses the point about having good-quality hosting. If a virus or piece of malware goes searching for back doors and finds a server with lots on it, it will scour the websites hosted there.

One week later the problem was back, with Google reporting once again that there was a threat to anyone accessing this website. This was due to the hosting having remained on the original server and because we had only accessed the CMS and not the site files. At this point we managed to get access to the actual site files. To prevent further problems we evaluated the files, renamed those that were not needed and locked them all down. We also moved the hosting to a much cleaner server, the site was resubmitted and was fully functional again overnight.

IF YOU FIND YOURSELF IN THIS SITUATION...

Don't panic; speak with your website designer first as they should be able to help in the same way we did in the above example. With any luck the virus or malware infection will be removed easily and the back doors will be shut. If your website designer cannot offer help then seek it from another website design agency that can. The problem will not go away on its own; leave it too long and restoring your website's status with the search engines will be all the more difficult.

Equally, if you have designed and built your own website then you can have a go at working it out, or find a website design agency that can help you. Ask in advance about their hourly rate; it should take an agency a few hours. Do bear in mind, though, how much you are losing not just in terms of enquiries but in your reputation by leaving it unsorted for even a day.

AVOIDING PROBLEMS IN FUTURE

It is a good idea to have a look at the host server and check whether or not any other websites on there have recently resulted in malicious software being downloaded and installed without user consent. Unfortunately there is no nice easy link or web page that I can find to give you – just this very non user-friendly one. This one shows my own domain name in the middle after the = sign; simply replace that with your own, ensuring there is no 'www.' and the end section is included:

http://www.google.com/safebrowsing/diagnostic?site=issl. co.uk#sthash.VknHDiYP.dpuf

It will tell you if anything looks to be of concern, and you can click on the link to the server if it is shown. This is the result from my own website and, as you can see, there is nothing suspicious.

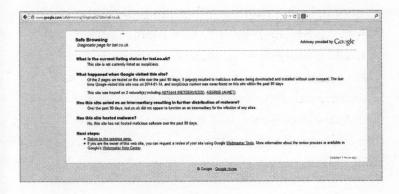

The safe browsing test screen

Again, with this book being printed in black and white it is a little tricky for you to tell, but what would be a blue link is for the servers that you can then link to, and you should get something like this:

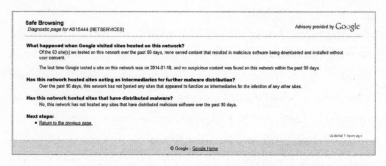

The safe browsing activity on the network on the server

TIP The sooner you can get it fixed the better. The message alone will put people off using your website and they will move on and look at the next in the list.

Once you are happy that all is sorted and you have told Google, then you (or ideally your web designer) need to submit the site to antivirus sites such as AVG and MacAfee and tell them that it is all fixed up. AVG tends to respond quite quickly.

9

DIY WEBSITES –
AND AVOIDING PITFALLS

As the owner of a website design agency, you would expect me to recommend that you always ask a professional to design and build a website for you to ensure that it is produced by someone who knows what they are doing and is thus fit for purpose. Indeed the same can be said of many businesses where there is a 'do it yourself' option. The attraction of DIY websites – or using a friend or family member who has done some design in the past and made the odd website – is that it will be free or cost very little. Remember that free or cheap is not always the best option, however, and that it is your business/reputation that is at stake if your website is not up to scratch.

IMPORTANT CONSIDERATIONS

DO YOU REALLY HAVE THE TIME?

As any small business owner will tell you, 'time is money'. Before you embark on designing and building your own website, work out your hourly rate and how long it will take you and compare that with a specialist web design agency's charges. In most cases your time would be better spent marketing, selling and running your own business. On average it takes one of my designers a minimum of twenty hours to design and build a five-to-seven-page website to a unique design (not a template), integrated into a CMS, all tested to comply with relevant legal regulations and work in all web browsers. It does not, however, include time for adding the content and optimizing said content for the search engines. Thus your hourly rate has to be quite low to be worth it, and you need to be as quick – and as good.

WILL YOUR FRIEND/FAMILY MEMBER BE ABLE TO MANAGE YOUR WEBSITE IN THE FUTURE?

This is the most common problem that I come across: a business owner who has been offered a free website by someone who is not currently working full time – or perhaps a student – usually a friend of a friend who is looking to improve their portfolio and get started. The person doing the work is creative and knows enough about the relevant online tools to build a website, and in some cases have learnt HTML and will build directly in code. They will usually offer to do it for very little, or for free. This may sound ideal when starting out or if you have a very small business, as cash flow is always difficult.

The problem arises when that person either finishes their studies or moves, or becomes fully employed and so no longer has time to help you out and make necessary changes to your website when required. This can cause major problems for the business owner; an out-of-date and inaccurate website is worse than no website at all, and will remain in that state until a design agency gets involved and rescues the site or the owner starts all over again.

UNDERSTANDING WEBSITE LEGISLATION

Chapter 3 looked in detail at the legislation with which your website must comply. Designing and building your own website because you are creative and to keep costs down is one thing; building a website to ensure compliance and meet with current standards is quite another. The same problem can arise when a graphic designer embarks on building their creation — an architect would never build a property that they have designed, so why would you expect a graphic designer to build your website? Design is part of the job, but building a website is a specialist role. Once you know what legislation you need to comply with, you need to understand how to build to comply with it.

FAILURE TO COMPLY WITH THE EU COOKIE DIRECTIVE

If your website does not comply with the EU Cookie Directive, someone can report you to the Information Commissioner's Office (ICO) in the UK and you can be forced to amend your website or instructed to pull it down. If you have been found to be collecting data without the end user's consent, then technically you could be in breach of the Data Protection Act. Since it is so easy to comply with the Directive there really is little excuse not to do so.

FAILURE TO COMPLY WITH THE EQUALITY ACT

This is essential. At the end of the day (in the vast majority of cases) it is easy to make reasonable effort with your website design and build to make it usable for a visually impaired person using a screen reader. If the website builder does not make reasonable effort to do this, they could be reported for discrimination. You will be given the opportunity to rectify the situation quickly before any further action is taken against you. As of June 2013, the RNIB state that they are unaware of any case having been brought to court in the UK, although they did start legal proceedings against BMI Baby over its failure to deal with the poor accessibility of its website. Its pressure resulted in BMI making changes.

As already mentioned, complicity is very easy to achieve and much of it relates to professional standards and simple things such as naming images, ensuring forms can be accessed by a screen reader with the correct tab orders, using decent-sized fonts from the outset and colours that do not clash or contrast in a way that makes it difficult for partially sighted readers. The Equality Act is 'anticipatory' which means that the onus is on you to think ahead and to ensure that when you make changes these conditions are still met. You cannot plead ignorance as a defence, even going forward when you make your own changes using a content management system.

CHOOSING THE CONTENT MANAGEMENT SYSTEM OR ONLINE TOOL

THE DIY OPTION

There are many free or cheap online options available to help you if you want to do this yourself, many of which are not based in the UK. Some companies offering such website solutions are focusing on price, hoping that you sign up at a low-cost monthly rate and then never get around to cancelling the card payment, despite not actually using the tools that they give you. This does not apply to all online companies, obviously, and if you do have the time and ability then go for it.

If you look at using website tools from companies such as Mywebsite.issl, 1 and 1, Weebly, etc, you get access to an online tool to build your own site. You pick a template from their selections and then add your own logo, change the colour scheme and add your own text. You will be able to add your own pages as you go along and customize the template to your personal style. You can make the template look very good with your own images and information.

There are, however, some important things to think about:

- Does your chosen tool give you the option to add your own SEO information to each page? Since the major search engines do not use keywords, a field for these could be seen as pointless.
- Things such as title tags (see Chapter 6) are crucial to help your website be found among the millions of others that are out there; can you add them?

- Are you able to add a description tag to each page to tell the search engines what the page is about?
- Can you give each page its own friendly URL, or does it have to be a default one that is not optimized?
- If the tool is an American one, does it give you the tools to comply with the EU Cookie Directive? You may assume it will, but why? This is an EU regulation.
- Are you given the option to describe any images and logos added? If not, then compliance with the Equality Act could prove difficult.
- Is the website transferable at any point? In most cases the answer is no. This means that if you want to hand it over to any design agency to make changes or improve it as your business grows and gets busier, there is a good chance that it will not be possible and you will need to start over.
- Have you got access to the HTML code? You may not need this but, going forward, it does mean that you have fewer restrictions than without it.

NOTE On the subject of the Equality Act, many of these tools do not give you access to the back-end files. This means that if you run your website through one of the basic checking systems and faults are found with the code, then it is likely that you will not be able to make the necessary changes. It won't be a case of asking a designer to do it for you as they will not have access either. The standards that these tools use are not necessarily the most current; at the end of the day they are the cheap or free option and you get what you pay for.

WORDPRESS

I covered this when talking about content management systems in Chapter 1. When deciding to design and build their own website, many people will go down this route as it is well known and there are many free downloads and templates, and many additional widgets to help personalize it. Once the website is designed and built, you can ask any hosting company for space and transfer the files over to their server.

Using WordPress does mean that any website design agency can pick it up at any point and help with it, as and when you grow and no longer have the time. The downside, however, is that it is primarily designed for blogging so the website structure can be based on articles rather than pages. Naturally with a good template it can all be worked around, as long as you know what the terminology means, where to look and what to enter where.

Some of the templates are very good indeed and others less so; think carefully and choose the right one for ease of use by you. As with the online tools mentioned earlier the template designers for WordPress all have their own styles and standards and you need to ensure that you have got a SEO module included. These are usually separate from the initial download template, but by searching in the help file you should be able to find the module and install it. Once installed you may find that the home page of the site has SEO tools in a different place to the rest of the articles/pages.

When uploading images to the site, make sure that they are resized beforehand to ensure that the website is not slow in loading, and that they are all named and given an 'alternate' text for a screen reader.

WordPress websites are common and in many cases you can tell a business has opted for one of their templates. This is perfectly acceptable – unless you want to show off your individuality, of course.

OTHER OPTIONS

The above options are probably the most common but there are others available online, many of which are open source (i.e. free). Most also come with free templates (as well as paid-for ones), but you do need to have the patience to read through the help and instructions and ensure that you have included all the elements that are required. Always remember that there is much more involved in making your web presence work for you, your business and your customers than just having a nice-looking website.

CAN YOU DESIGN A MOBILE-FRIENDLY VERSION?

So you have set up your own website online, started the design using a free template, allocated the time to alter the colour scheme and logo. You have entered your own images and started adding the relevant content, and have even remembered to include the headings and subheadings for the search engines.

Did you remember to see if the template came with a mobile-friendly version included? If not, all is not lost, as you may be able to design a mobile version yourself, but to be honest this is not that easy. Mobile-friendly websites are specifically designed to work on a number of smartphone screen sizes and the biggest difference is usually in navigation. While a desktop site is landscape and more often than not in widescreen, a mobile version is portrait and so the fundamental part of the website – the navigation – must have two options: horizontal and vertical. If you can't make your chosen template do this then find a template that can. It will not be long before the search engines start basing their results on the end user's device, and if your website is not suitable then you could miss out on leads and therefore business.

DO YOU HAVE THE TOOLS FOR TESTING YOUR WEBSITE?

When the website is designed and built you have the job of testing it to ensure that what you can see, your customers and potentially new customers can also see. You can of course download the current versions of the most common web browsers, i.e. Google Chrome, Mozilla Firefox and Internet Explorer, not forgetting Apple Mac users and their own browser Safari. If you are a Windows user you will need to download a Safari emulator; if a Mac user you will need to find an Internet Explorer emulator. You then need to access an iPad, an Android tablet, a Windows tablet and maybe even a Kindle HD Fire to ensure that the handheld devices being used to access the web on the move can all access your website. Tablets don't require mobile-friendly versions as the screens are larger and the normal rule of thumb is that a traditional desktop website should work on one.

Having the four main web browsers and access to the tablets will cover most users, but the statistics show that many visitors to your website – potential customers – will be using older versions of the leading browsers. There are emulators available online that will replicate these versions, so ideally you need to find these, download them and test your website in them. These emulators are not necessarily free, although some may have a free trial option. Remember that problems may arise if you do not have access to all the back-end files and so cannot amend certain necessary elements.

LANGUAGES

The languages used to build a website are mentioned in Appendix 1 and also covered in Chapter 5.

In most cases, if you are building your own website you will probably use one of the tools mentioned above, but if you are going to build using code I would suggest opting for HTML5. This is current and very efficient, and there are lots of books available to teach you how to use it, in easy lessons.

10
YOU HAVE YOUR WEBSITE –
NOW WHAT?

Whether you have built your own website or had a design agency do it for you, once it is live and hosted you need to think about what happens next. As already mentioned, a content management system that you can use is essential for its future management. A well-built website will technically last you a fair amount of time but paying for it and then just leaving it sitting on the internet with the odd text update is not making the best use of it. Remember that your website will often be the first impression any new client will get of you so make sure that, going forward, your web presence continues to win new customers – you can do this by maintaining your website properly, much as you do your car.

THINK OF YOUR CAR...

A new car is an essential part of your life, especially when it comes to visiting clients or suppliers. All nice and new and working at its best, all you need to do is add fuel and top up the water every now and again. To ensure that it keeps running efficiently, however, you will book it in with a garage to have it serviced on a regular basis. Some car owners will lift the bonnet and change spark plugs or the oil themselves, but in reality most people are not mechanics and have very little idea of what needs to be looked at, let alone what to actually do with it. So your new pride and joy will be booked into a garage where the expert mechanics will look it over and adjust and tweak anything that needs it. The mechanic will test brakes and tyres and assess what (if any) wear and tear has taken place and advise you accordingly.

Now think of the website that you have just had designed and built for your business. You have paid for this nice new essential business tool and have been on the ball and made content changes, and added some news and maybe even a blog or two, but have you lifted the bonnet? Have you looked at the nuts and bolts that are keeping the website working for your business? Behind the scenes is the back-end system that allows you to update small things easily but it too needs servicing; it needs to be checked to see if the engine is working at its most efficient level, and tested to see if it will work on any technology that has been launched or updated since it was built. For example, many people will have experienced the situation where a smartphone releases an update and suddenly things no longer work and you end up with lots of updates of applications. Similarly the release of the latest Windows operating system is usually followed by an update by the main web browsers (Internet Explorer, Google Chrome, Mozilla Firefox) to work with it. Your website is crucial to your business so getting a regular service is essential. Regular checking and maintenance will ensure that the website is running as efficiently as it can and that you, your business and your customers are getting the best from it.

SERVICING

Sticking with the car analogy, a garage will normally check the oil, tyres, brakes, run some engine diagnostics and give it a wash, and if you're lucky a mini valet. A similar service can be arranged with your web design agency. Note that if the web design agency or individual website designer who designed and built the website does not offer an aftercare service system or payment plan, this doesn't mean that you can't have one. As with a car, the garage you bought it from may not be the same one you take it to for servicing.

HOW OFTEN SHOULD MY WEBSITE BE SERVICED?

This can depend on the aftercare packages being offered and the size and usage of a website (some car services are based on mileage rather than time – the bigger the site the more that may be needed). It also depends on what is included in the aftercare; there may be elements that are included that are not about a regular service but more to do with performance, and making sure that the website is not just running at its best and working with all current technologies but also working in terms of SEO. Whatever you decide upon, it should be serviced annually at the very least.

WHAT WILL MY WEBSITE SERVICE INCLUDE?

Different website design agencies will offer different aftercare and service options. As a guideline there should always be some basic tests and checks included; it then depends on the size and complexity of the website. A small five-page website for a hair salon, for example, will require much less servicing than an e-commerce shop selling hundreds of products. Below is a list of things that should be checked, and some of the extra options that I would expect to be included.

- **Health check** A health check will determine what needs to be looked at and fixed, where necessary; without this you will not know what requires updating.
- **Updates to the content management software** The software providers and developers will update their own back-end system on a regular basis to ensure that it keeps up to date with changing technology, in the same way that Windows or Apple updates. The difference is you cannot update automatically as this could stop the website working because there are many other elements to take into account, such as additional modules that have been installed for news, calendars or social media widgets. If you update one element without checking compatibility with the others it may just all stop working.
- **Updates to the CMS modules** All websites have different elements and tools that are used on them, for example some websites have a calendar or a blog module whereas others do not. Every module installed into the CMS will be updated by the particular developer who created it and thus updating will be required to ensure that everything is compatible.

- **Changes to text and images** This is a good time to get those updates made that you have not had time to do; not just text, but maybe a refresh of images.

- **Check the SEO** If you have been changing text and images throughout the site, have you amended the SEO accordingly? This check will assess what has changed on all pages.

- **Amend title tags for relevance** Once the pages have been checked, the actual changes need to be made to ensure that the title tags tie in with the content on the site and that it is up to date and relevant.

- **Amend page headings for relevance** Have the necessary heading tags been amended to tie in with the new content on specific pages?

- **Create friendly URLs or amend existing ones where necessary** If you have changed the content or your target market, the original URLs may need amending to suit.

- **Amend the Meta descriptions** When the content has been amended the page description also needs to be changed.

- **Amend the footer information** Footers are very useful areas for SEO but here too the information must be consistent with general page and site content. Ensuring that this is updated on a regular basis will also help with the website SEO.

- **Removal of dead pages** Some business owners start off with very good intentions of updating news on their websites (and are sure that they will have time to do it); the same goes for testimonials and blogs etc. This cleanse allows for the removal of pages that have not been updated, or for them to be replaced with something more useful.

- **Changes to pages within the website** If you want to remove a service and add a new one, for example, now is the time to do it. Equally some services will include a set number of new pages that can be added at the same time.

- **Compatibility check with browsers** This will test the website to ensure that any changes that have been made to the main web browsers have not stopped any element of your website from working properly. It will usually include the fixes needed to make it work.

- **Compatibility check with the iPad** This will test the website to ensure that any changes that have been made to the tablet and its operating system have not affected the way in which your website is displayed. Where there are any issues the technician will more than likely be able to fix it.

- **Compliance check with legislation** This will ensure that your website is compliant with any new rules. Also make sure that any content changes or new images have been done with the Equality Act in mind; check that you have not inadvertently caused the site to no longer comply on the basics. You may have added a social media feed into the site such as a video and not realized that it may now need a privacy policy and cookie pop-up in order to comply with the EU Cookie Directive. All this can be fixed now.

- **Compatibility check with current standards** Technology develops at a very quick pace. This test will check – if twelve months on – that the website still meets the standards, and if not will fix it to ensure it does.

- **Performance check** I am guilty of not checking my own website's performance often enough. If someone emailed me a short report of information on a regular basis, I would definitely look at it and make changes and improvements based on that very important data. A service may also give you that data, not always with Google Analytics but via the server's own data (which may be more informative as it will include other search engines).

> **Tip** If you take a service plan with a website design agency, there is a very good chance that it will also include the hosting and a number of associated email accounts as part of the package.

HOW MUCH IS A SERVICE LIKELY TO COST?

Reverting back to the car analogy, the cost of the service will depend on how much work is needed. There will be a fixed price for the service and then further charges for parts and labour. The same is true with a website, although there will not usually be a cost for parts (sometimes in complex websites new modules may have to be paid for) but certainly for labour as the above work does take a lot of time. The longer a website has been running without being serviced, the greater the chance of more remedial work being required, and thus the first may be more expensive than future services. If the website consists of just five pages and one or two modules, this will be much cheaper than a twenty-page website with news, calendars, social media integrations and blogs.

Prevention is better than cure

We have our cars serviced and maintained to help prevent a nasty and often expensive problem occurring in the future. Treat your website in the same way: if one of the web browsers decides to release a new version and your website doesn't work with it, then some of your clients and potential clients may not be able to use it. Would you know that this was the case? You probably wouldn't unless you have the time to keep an eye on all changes from all browsers and then further time to download them and check the site against them. A regular check-up and service will minimize any major impact from changes that are outside the website.

AFTERCARE PLAN

An aftercare plan is very similar to a car service plan that many major garages now offer. Many web design agencies will offer an aftercare plan where you pay a fixed monthly sum and are not then presented with a larger bill in one go (helpful with that all-important cash flow). The cost per month will vary but could start from as little as £25 plus VAT depending on the size and complexity of the website. It is advisable to start the aftercare plan as soon as your new website is built, so that when the time comes for its first service you know that you are covered.

If your website is a few years old but you still like the site design and have no desire to change it, then getting a health check is a good idea and will give you the opportunity to assess what remedial work (if any) is required and how to progress from there.

CHANGING YOUR WEBSITE

Even with maintenance and regular servicing, a car will get to a point where the maintenance outweighs its value, or it is simply no longer fit for purpose due to changes in circumstances. It could be that you are bored of the style and want something different, or that newer cars have gadgets that were not available when you bought yours.

The same is true of your website; a new one will be needed at some point, when the changes and updates required make it more cost-effective to do so. It could be that you are looking to rebrand and are changing your marketing campaigns, or that you simply want a change of style and design and thus a fresh launch. If you have regularly maintained your website there is a good chance that the same content can be reused, thus helping to speed up a new build. A website redesign involves a rebuild and budgeting this for every three or four years is not a bad idea.

A new website is also a good public-relations opportunity and will still be one of the most cost-effective marketing methods for any business.

APPENDIX 1
GLOSSARY OF TERMS

JARGON BUSTING

This glossary covers a number of the main words and abbreviations that website designers and developers may use either in face-to-face discussion or in any written proposals. It is not an exhaustive list but should cover the basics.

Analytics Record details of visitor traffic to your website; not just how many people click, but how long they stay, which website browser they are using, whether it was from a mobile device, which pages they spent the longest time on and so on. The most commonly used form is Google Analytics.

ASP A Microsoft product and an alternative to PHP (see page 152); a language used to build database-driven websites that are then hosted on a Windows server.

Back end Used to describe accessing the website through an administration system with a login rather than looking at a website on the internet as a user.

Browsers Used to browse internet pages; the most common are Google Chrome, Mozilla Firefox, Internet Explorer (IE) and Safari.

Cache A way of saying your local computer has stored a copy of the website in its memory. It helps speed up the loading of regularly used websites, but you may need to clear it if you are not seeing some updates.

CMS (Content Management System) Allows an end user to login and edit content and information on their own website as and when required.

Control Panel (cPanel) Where a user has a login and can access their domain name (.abc.com) and make changes; also from where emails can sometimes be accessed.

Cookies A piece of data that is transferred from a website to your web browser and stored there for future use. Websites that use logins use cookies to save the end user having to repeatedly enter their username.

Database-driven Some website content is driven by a database that changes on a regular basis, for example an estate or letting agent, where the properties being marketed are held in a database and used as part of a property search, or flagged as a featured property and then sent to property portals for them to display on their site.

Domain name The letters and numbers following 'www.'; e.g. the BBC's domain name is bbc.co.uk.

E-commerce A shopping cart website where products can be added to a 'basket' and you can pay online.

Front end The opposite of back end; used to describe someone using the website traditionally through a web browser.

FTP (File Transfer Protocol) A way of transferring files between a local computer and a website server.

Hosting Storing a website on a computer that the world can access via the internet.

HTML (Hypertext Markup Language) The main language used when creating web pages that can be displayed via a web browser.

HTML5 The most current language used to design and build websites.

IP (address) (Internet Protocol) The address is a numerical value given to the location of a user's computer or network. IP addresses are used in tracking where things are and in some cases the computer or network something was done from.

JS (Java Script) A computer programming language, used in the development of websites rather than the design.

Keywords/key phrases What you and your business want to be found under via search engines; e.g. a travel agent in Preston would use the words 'Travel agent, Preston' in various places in the website text and the designer would use the same words in the titles.

Nominet One of the world's leading internet registry companies, based in the UK and focusing on .uk domain names; its members agree to abide by their good practices.

Payment gateway The provider chosen to handle online payments on e-commerce websites; e.g. PayPal, World Pay, SAGE and Payment Sense etc.

PHP A programming language that is used to build more complex websites requiring special functionality.

Responsive (website) An increasingly popular term for a website that responds to the size of screen on which it is being viewed. In most cases this is the same as being 'mobile-friendly' but this goes further in that it will scale to fit intermediate sizes such as tablets.

SEO (Search Engine Optimisation) A way of helping a website appear higher on search engines such as Google, Bing or Yahoo.

SSL (Secure Sockets Layer) Needed for some websites if online payments are being taken.

URL Link appearing at the top of the web page when it opens up, e.g. the English news section of the BBC is www.bbc.co.uk/news/england.

Validation Websites are built to certain standards set by the World Wide Web Consortium (see page 153); validation checks that the website code conforms with these.

W3C (World Wide Web Consortium) An international community where member organisations, a full-time staff and the public work together to develop web standards.

XHTML (Extensible Hypertext Markup Language) Another member of the family of languages in which web pages are written.

XML (Extensible Markup Language) A variant of language used for encoding documents that both humans and computers can read.

APPENDIX 2
USEFUL REFERENCES AND LINKS

Throughout this book I have referred to a number of free and general online tools that can be helpful when checking elements of your website. I have also included links to some informative content resources online. The basic ones listed here should allow you to check your own website and see where it stands in the general scheme of things.

Google's YouTube Channel Matt Cutts posts videos regularly on the subject of SEO in plain English. They are usually less than three minutes long and well worth subscribing to so that you can keep up to date with the changes.
• http://www.youtube.com/user/GoogleWebmasterHelp

W3C This is more for those who want to delve into the technical world of development, but still a very useful resource for factual information.
• http://www.w3.org

W3C Validator A useful free tool where you can enter your URL and check your own website for any errors and get an instant report.
• http://validator.w3.org/

Cynthia Says One of the very good free online tools for getting the basic checks done on your website to ensure compliance with the Equality Act. **Note:** If you use this, change the default from Section 508 to WCAG 2.0 AAA.

• http://www.cynthiasays.com/

Wave Web Accessibility Evaluation Tool An alternative to Cynthia and just as good; it simply displays the data in a different way.

• http://wave.webaim.org/

ICO Information Commissioners' Office For further information on the EU Cookies Directive and how it affects you and your website.

• http://www.ico.org.uk/for_organisations/privacy_and_electronic_communications/the_guide/cookies

Google Webmaster Tools You will need to create an account but it is free and you can then add your website and start using all the tools at your disposal.

• http://www.google.com/webmasters/tools/

Google Places Again you need to register; there is a verification process and it is not always instant. If you have an automated telephone system, use your mobile number to register as the process is automated and the two don't work well together.

• http://www.google.co.uk/business/placesforbusiness/

ISSL My website design agency that will help with free advice wherever possible.
- http://www.issl.co.uk
- http://mywebsite.issl.co.uk

Website Browser Emulator Browserstack is one option for testing your website in a variety of versions of Internet Explorer, Firefox, Chrome, Safari and Opera, and across a number of platforms, not just Windows.
- http://www.browserstack.com/list-of-browsers-and-platforms

What's My IP When you go to this website it will look at where you are and show you your IP address.
- http://whatismyipaddress.com/?u=TRUE

You Get Signal A great quick tool telling you who else is on the same server as your website. Simply enter the URL (without the www.) and click check. A full list of sites will appear and you can click through to look at the standards on the server you are sharing.
- http://www.yougetsignal.com/tools/web-sites-on-web-server/

APPENDIX 3
SOURCES AND
ACKNOWLEDGEMENTS

In addition to useful links in Appendix 2, some of the examples used throughout the book have been screenshots of a variety of websites, some small and some internationally recognized. Without the ability to show how large international organizations use the internet and make the most from their websites, it would have been quite hard to demonstrate how this works for the smaller businesses. Google, the BBC and the Wikipedia websites are open and the content can be used freely. These are all great examples of excellent websites, which I would like to acknowledge here. I would also like to thank the small business owners for letting me use screenshots of their own websites to help explain in pictures some of the more wordy bits.

Thanks are also due to:

- Amanda MacDougall from AM Accounting Services of Burnley, Lancashire
- Dale Connern of Dansworks Dance Academy in Bacup, Lancashire
- Emma Farrow of Farrow and Farrow Estate Agents in Rawtenstall, Rossendale, Lancashire
- ISSL website design and development agency, Lancashire
- Langford Rae Estate Agents of Sevenoaks, Kent
- Visit Rossendale, the official tourist website for Rossendale, Lancashire
- Anthony J Turner Estate and Letting Agents in Hebden Bridge, West Yorkshire.

INDEX

Plans and tables are in *italics*
Items in the glossary are in **bold**